# "YES" or "NO"

## THE GUIDE TO BETTER DECISIONS

# Spencer Johnson

HarperCollins*Publishers*
HarperBusiness

For my wife, Lesley

### NOTE:

This First Edition of *"YES" or "NO"* contains a streamlined two-question "YES" or "NO" System to provide readers of this book with a more useful and memorable way to make better decisions, compared with the original six-question system which appeared in an earlier Advance Edition of this book. Other modifications have been made, based on valuable feedback from readers of the Advance Edition, including how the System can be used in groups. The content, however, is essentially the same in both editions.

A hardcover edition of this book was published in 1992 by HarperCollins Publishers.

HarperCollins books may be purchased for educational, business, or sales promotional use. For information, please call or write: Special Markets Department, HarperCollins Publishers, Inc. 10 East 53rd Street, New York, NY 10022.

First HarperPerennial edition published 1993.

LIBRARY OF CONGRESS CATALOG CARD NUMBER FOR THE HARDCOVER EDITION 91-57929

ISBN 0-88730-631-4(pbk.)

95 96 98 99 00 RRD 10 9 8 7 6 5 4 3

## *Introduction*

In 1986, it became clear to me that too many of us were making a series of poor decisions in this country. We were losing our world position in commerce, living in a deteriorating environment, experiencing a rising crime rate, and seeing the effects of drug use, divorce, and homelessness. Whether we wanted to see it or not, we were probably in the position we were in, in large part, due to the decisions we were collectively making.

I wondered, "Where had so many of us gone wrong and what could we do about it? Could we learn to make better decisions on our own and enjoy better results in our work and our personal lives? And if enough of us made better decisions in our own lives, could we, together, create better businesses, better communities, and better families?"

When most of us look at our lives, we can see, with hindsight, some of the mistakes we have made. Knowing that no one wants to make a poor decision, I began to study how we make decisions and discovered what became obvious: Our poor decisions were based on illusions we believed at the time, and our better decisions, on realities we recognized in time.

After several years of studying, I discovered what I trust you will discover while reading this story: a reliable system of knowing how to say "Yes" to what works well for each of us and "No" to what doesn't.

If you find this system is useful to you, I hope you will help other people discover how to use it as well.

*Spencer Johnson*

# Acknowledgments

This book is a collection of many insights gained from practical heads and generous hearts--some from books written long ago, others from contemporary conversations. I want to acknowledge several of these sources of wisdom including:

*Dr. DeWitt Baldwin,* Director of Medical Education Research and Information at the American Medical Association, for his insights into stress reduction through integrity.

*Dr. Paul Brenner,* for his concern in balancing thinking with feeling, and his insight into the body's binary code.

*Jim Cathcart* for his several valuable suggestions.

Filmmakers *Ray Christensen, John Christensen,* and *Brad Neal* of Charthouse International Learning and associate *Joel Suzuki* for their clarity, and for their emphasis on storytelling.

*Dr. Richard Farson* and associates at The Western Behavioral Sciences Institute for inviting me to participate on their international computer network of Business Executives and for their analysis of the concepts in this book.

All the talented people at *HarperCollins Publishers,* for their most valuable contributions.

*Matthew Juechter* for his guidance on how the "Yes" or "No" System can be used in organizations.

*Margret McBride* of the McBride Literary Agency, for her personal insights and essential help with this book.

*Nevins McBride* for his practical business applications.

*Dr. Carl Rogers* for what he taught me about the wisdom that resides in each person.

*Marshall Thurber* for his focus on a reliable System.

And, finally, to the large number of business executives and community leaders who read the manuscript and the First Advance Edition and who gave suggestions based on their own experiences with making better decisions. Their practical experiences and suggestions were invaluable.

✓
# *Contents*

## From Confusion to Clarity

There was once a bright young man who was looking for a way to make good decisions--to have more success and less stress in his life.

Although he did not make many poor decisions, when he did, they created problems for him at work and occasionally caused upheavals in his private life.

He felt his poor decisions were costing him too much, and he sensed there must be a better way.

So, he set out for the nearby mountains one day, in the early morning light, to join other businesspeople on The Hike, a renowned weekend experience led by "the guide," an extraordinary businessman and hiker who guided people through the mountains and through their decisions.

The young man heard that people had discovered a reliable system of decision making, and had returned from these weekends able to make better decisions.

But how had they learned to use it so well in such a short time?

Later, as the young man hiked along the trail at the foot of the mountain, he took off his light jacket and tied it around his waist. He was sweating now, not from the morning sunshine, but because he felt anxious. He knew he was late and lost.

Soon after he left home, he realized that he had forgotten the directions to the camp. Now he wished he had gone back for them, but he thought then that it might make him a little late, so he hadn't taken the time. Now very late, he proceeded in the same direction but at a much faster pace.

The young man consoled himself that he was not the only person who needed to make better decisions. He had been a part of several business groups whose decisions were, at best, mediocre.

The results of poor decisions were evident everywhere people made decisions: in corporations, in small businesses, in schools, in government agencies, and, too often, in people's personal lives.

It was as though people made no connection between their own choices and the consequences.

The young man wondered why so many smart people so often made dumb decisions.

He began to criticize himself. He didn't always know how to work as a decisive member of a group or team. He knew sometimes he was indecisive. He just didn't want to make mistakes. Then he realized that he, like most people, had never been taught how to make decisions.

At that moment, he stepped on a dry twig and the sharp sound snapped him back to his surroundings. He stopped and looked around.

It was then that he saw the other man.

For a moment, the two men eyed one another cautiously until the young man noticed that the older man's tanned face seemed to radiate clarity. He wondered whether this tall, gray-haired, fit-looking gentleman could be the guide. For some reason, the young man felt safer in the stranger's presence. "I am looking for The Hike," he said.

The older man responded, "I am your guide. You are headed in the wrong direction." Then he turned and the young man followed him.

The guide looked back over his shoulder and said, "You might do well to look at the decisions that made you late today." The embarrassed young man said nothing, but he started to look at his decisions.

Later, the guide asked, "Why have you come on The Hike?"

The young man answered, "I want to learn how to make the best decisions." As he said it, he could feel the familiar pressure of having to figure out what was best. He knew this sometimes made him indecisive because he didn't know what was good enough.

As he walked along, the guide said, "Perhaps you do not always need to make the best decisions. For things to get better, we only need to make *better* decisions. Perhaps, like the rest of us, you will find that if you just keep making better decisions, eventually you will do well."

The young man felt a sense of relief. "May I ask what you mean by a 'better' decision?"

"A better decision is one that makes us feel better --about *how* we make it--and that gets better *results*.

"By 'a better decision,'" the guide said, "I mean a better decision than we would have made if we had not asked ourselves a couple of valuable questions.

"Perhaps, you, at times, like many other people, feel that you are indecisive or that you make half-decisions--ones you feel may not be good enough.

"Many of us you will meet on this hike overcame that feeling by using a reliable system of doing two things--using our heads and consulting our hearts--to soon arrive at a better decision. Part of this system consists of asking ourselves two valuable questions, which we answer either 'Yes' or 'No'."

The young man immediately asked, "What are the two questions?"

"Before we get to the questions, shall we start our journey at the beginning?" the guide asked.

When the young man agreed, the guide asked, "As you look ahead to making a better decision, do you know what you need to do first?"

"I'm not sure," the young man said.

"If you don't know what to do," the guide asked, "do you know what *not* to do?"

Usually, the young man was so busy doing so many things, he didn't think about what *not* to do.

Suddenly the guide stopped in his tracks.

And the young man stopped next to him.

The guide said, "You must simply stop doing whatever you are doing."

Then the guide pulled a folded piece of paper from his wallet and showed him a part of it.

After the young man read it, he thought about it, and then took out a small red journal from his backpack and wrote a note to himself:

✓

*To make a better decision,
I first stop
proceeding with a poor decision.*

✓

The guide said, "If you stop a poor decision and create a void, you can fill it with something better."

The young man said, "But I'm afraid that if I give up what I have, I won't find anything better."

"We are all afraid of that," the guide said. "It takes courage to let go of what is familiar and comfortable. But, in reality, it is actually a safer and more reliable way to get better results.

"When what is not working for you is finally out of your way, you are then free to find something better. And you usually do, rather quickly.

"The ancient Chinese had an expression for this wisdom. 'If you want a hot cup of tea, you must first empty your cup.' Pouring hot tea into a cup full of cold tea means the hot tea cannot enter the cup but rather spills over onto the saucer."

"I see," the young man said slowly. Then he offered, "That reminds me of a buyer friend of mine. He avoided firing an incompetent supplier, who had failed to perform satisfactorily after being given several chances. My friend knew of no one better to do the job, so instead of stopping what wasn't working, he continued using the same supplier."

"What happened?" the guide asked.

The young man said, "The supplier kept making mistakes and it cost my friend's company time and money. Eventually, it was my friend who was fired for not doing his job, I'm sorry to say."

The young man thought for a moment and then asked, "Why do we keep doing what we know doesn't work?"

"Because," the guide said, "although it is often dangerous, we feel safer if we do not change what is familiar. Eventually, the ineffective but familiar way becomes accepted. You see this in organizations."

"Can you give me an example?"

"Yes. Many years ago, the U.S. Army wanted to get off more rapid rounds of cannon fire and so hired a consultant to study the problem. He went into the field and noticed that the soldiers stepped back from the cannon and waited for about three seconds every time before they fired the cannon.

"When he asked why, they replied that they were following directions laid down in the army manual. The consultant read through all the back issues of the manual until he had traced the instructions to their origin in the Civil War when the soldiers were advised to step away from their weapons before firing so they could hold the gun horses' heads. Otherwise, the horses would bolt, jerking the cannons off target."

The young man grinned at the thought of people stepping back to hold the reins of horses that were no longer there.

The guide led the young man across a small stream. He glanced at his compass.

Then he continued, "When the soldiers realized this, they changed. But how many of us are holding on to something similar without realizing it?"

The young man asked, "Can I tell you about the decisions I need to make--at work and at home?"

"No," the guide said. "I don't mean to be rude, but your decisions are *yours*, not mine. You may want to focus on a business or personal decision you need to make, and apply what you learn this weekend to your decision and see if it works well for you.

"If you do, you will probably find that you can soon make your own better decision."

Then the guide asked, "If you wanted to drive West, and suddenly realized you were going East, what would you do?"

"Well, as soon as I saw I was going the wrong way, I would turn around and change my direction."

The guide agreed, "Of course. Our making better decisions involves us going in a better direction. Now to get directions, do you want to rely on others or have a good map with you that you can rely on?"

The young man said, "I'd prefer to have my own good map. I remember reading Winston Churchill's comment: 'Personally I am always ready to learn, although I do not always like being taught.'"

The guide smiled, "Me too. It is a challenge for us to find a better way on our own, but any of us can do it by using the 'Yes' or 'No' System."

"How do I know it will work for me?" he asked.

"Why don't you just use it and see for yourself?

"Talk with the others on The Hike. While they are all from different countries, they all have something in common--they use the System successfully.

"Meantime, you can begin with this inventory."

The older man handed him an envelope and quickened his step. "We are late. We only have a weekend, so we go at a fast pace," he said over his shoulder, expecting the young man to keep up.

Later, they rested on the trail and the young man read and used what the guide had given him.

## Making a Better Decision

A Private Five-Minute Inventory

### A Business or Personal Decision:
What is a problem for me--a situation at work or in my life
that I wish would improve?

### My Initial Decision Is to:    (I write in my initial decision now)
What am I going to do about it?
___ For now, I am going to do nothing.
___ I will do something, but I am not sure of what or when.
___ Maybe, I will do the following:

### My *Better* Decision Is to:    (I write this in at the end of The Hike)

✓

# A Reliable System

When the guide and the young man reached the camp, they joined the other hikers, shaking hands with five men and two women from Australia, Brazil, Germany, Japan, and the United States.

One of the hikers had made and passed out caps with a legend on them reading "Yes" or "No" and, in tiny print, "decisions . . . decisions . . . decisions." The young man felt he was going to have some fun.

Over a lunch of sandwiches and apples, and fresh water from a nearby stream, the group continued to discuss The Hike. "So, are we going to hike up the north face of the mountain?" "If we encounter ice on the north slope, what alternate trail will we use?"

Then someone asked, "Do we want a challenging climb or do we need a thoughtful hike?"

Before long, they made their decisions. They would hike up the gentle east slope that afternoon, rest at sunset, hike after dark, and camp that night, halfway up the mountain.

Then they would hike the more difficult top half of the mountain all day Saturday, enjoy a bonfire Saturday night, and descend Sunday after a dawn gathering at the summit.

The young man remarked, "For such a decisive group of people, they sure ask enough questions.

"Why were they doing that?" he asked.

"They were using the first half of the 'Yes' or 'No' System," the guide revealed.

"Can you tell me more?" the young man asked.

"Certainly. The 'Yes' or 'No' System is a two-part journey to arrive at a better decision. To get there, we look at both sides of a decision by asking ourselves two questions--a practical question and a private one--and then we soon make our decision."

The guide added, "The questions you just heard were variations of the practical question."

"How does the system work?"

"We make an initial decision in our normal way. Then we ask ourselves a head question and a heart question, listen to ourselves and to others, make a better decision and act on it."

"And it really works?" the young man asked.

"Yes. My first boss introduced it to me years ago.

"He needed all of us to make better decisions, without checking with him every time. When he talked with us, he discovered most of us believed in either using our heads or listening to our hearts when we made our decisions, but few of us did both. So he showed us the 'Yes' or 'No' System to make better decisions--sooner. We used it and it worked."

"What happened?" the young man asked.

"Many of us made better decisions and the company became more profitable. We received promotions and bonuses. But more importantly, for me, I learned to do something that has helped me to be happier and more successful throughout my life."

The young man wanted to know what it was.

"It is this," the guide said, and he showed the young man another section of the same folded piece of paper from his wallet. It read:

✓

I avoid indecision and half-decisions
based on half-truths.

I use _both_ parts of a reliable system
to consistently make better decisions:
a cool head and a warm heart.

I USE MY HEAD
by asking myself a practical question
_and_
I CONSULT MY HEART
by asking myself a private question.

Then, after I listen to myself and others,
I make a better decision and act on it.

✓

"The key is to use a reliable system," the guide noted, "because the system produces consistently better results, even if mistakes are sometimes made. A mistake is never a flaw in the person, but in the system of thinking he or she is using."

The young man said, "That reminds me of what W. E. Deming said--the man whose system some credit with Japan's economic prosperity. He said, 'Eighty-five percent of all failure is in the system.'"

"I agree with him," the guide said. He pulled out suntan lotion, applied it to his face and hands, and offered to share it. Then they talked, out of the sun, under the shade of a large pine tree.

"The 'Yes' or 'No' System," the guide continued, "helps  people to look at what they say 'Yes' to and what they say 'No' to."

"I'm just beginning to realize," the young man said, "that where I am in life is largely the result of all the choices I've made." Then he smiled, "I think I could use a better system."

The guide smiled and said, "We all could.  In today's changing world, we all need to make better decisions, faster, just to survive, let alone prosper.

"And the better the system, the easier it is to avoid mistakes and to get consistently better results."

The guide added, "It is like a successful restaurant chain whose fast-food system lets a wide variety of workers all get the same consistently tasty results the customer comes to rely on and look forward to.

"Similarly, our employees who used the 'Yes' or 'No' System made fewer mistakes and got better results when they used it.  But the key is to use it."

The young man asked, "How do I use it?"

"You can use it in various ways. After making an initial decision, you can make a better decision by using your head or consulting your heart in any order you like. Both the head and the heart questions each have three ideas embedded in them. You will probably find that one or two of the ideas will be the most useful to you. These will be the few areas you feel you need to look at in a particular situation, or during a certain phase of your own life.

"Once you have learned the System, it becomes a mental circle you can enter at any point. Essentially, you can begin with either question, in any order, as long as you use *both* to arrive at a better decision."

"How much time does this usually take?" the young man wanted to know.

"That depends on how important the decision is to you and how clear you are. You can focus on one part of a question, which may help you to make a better decision in just a few minutes. Or you can spend more time, ask all three parts of both questions, and make an even better decision."

The young man admitted, "I'm afraid I haven't always been willing to take the time."

"That's true for most of us," the guide said. "But the more often you ask the head question and the heart question, the faster and the easier it becomes. When it becomes a habit, as it will, it is quite fast."

"What are the questions?"

The guide answered, "Ask the other hikers to tell you the questions during The Hike, and to explain their own personal experiences with them.

"Then," he suggested, "take a decision you need to make and really ask yourself the two questions.

"Afterwards, you might find you have made one of your own better decisions."

The guide cautioned, "Be patient in the beginning. You may think that half of this system is either too familiar to you or, perhaps, not important to you.

"But when you go back and forth over 'the bridge' you will learn about, you will experience both halves of yourself, and you will find what you are looking for. You will be able to make better decisions, either on your own or as a member of any group you are a part of--at work or at home."

The guide added, "Just remember to use *both* parts of the System. One won't work without the other."

Later, as they hiked up the gentle slope, the young man noticed the guide studying the paper he had taken from his wallet and had fully unfolded. "May I ask what you're looking at?"

"Certainly. It is my 'Yes' or 'No' Map. Many of us have made a written summary of the insights and the questions in the 'Yes' or 'No' System, which we call 'The Map'. I refer to it briefly when I want to reach a better decision. The beauty of The Map is that it reminds me how to find my own way."

The young man asked, "May I see it?"

"It may be better for you," the guide suggested, "if you learn how to make your own map while you are on The Hike. Then it will be more useful to you."

All of a sudden, the guide leaped to one side as they both heard a sound in the underbrush. He said, "Walk around the snake. It's poisonous."

The young man wondered how the guide had spotted the snake so quickly. He decided to pay extra attention to where he was going this weekend.

With that, the guide encouraged the young man to join the other hikers. Then the guide went off briefly to think on his own.

## √
## *The Real Need*

$A$s the hikers began their climb up the mountain, the young man found himself next to Franklin Neal, a brusque man from Chicago.

Neal was chairman of a major corporation and an important member of several other boards. He had learned about The Map eleven years before, and had used it successfully ever since.

He offered his firm hand and said gruffly, "Call me Frank." He looked straight ahead up the trail.

The young man had the feeling that this man didn't often invite people to use his first name.

The older man asked, "Is our talking about decisions going to be a waste of time for both of us? Or are you going to *use* what you learn?"

The young man replied, "Whatever I learn, I'm going to use it for a real decision I need to make.

"To get straight to the point," the young man said, "the guide told me that there are two questions that I can ask myself to help me make a better decision. What are the two questions?"

Frank said, "You can use your head by asking the first question:

*"Am I Meeting the Real Need, Informing Myself of Options, and Thinking It Through?"*

Frank suggested, "Ask yourself now. Are you?"

The young man answered quickly, "Sort of."

Frank boomed back, "Young man, wouldn't it help you if you could answer either 'Yes' or 'No'?"

The young man was startled. Then he grinned, turned his new cap around, and said, "Maybe."

Frank laughed out loud and it broke the ice. He knew the young man was uncertain and a little defensive, but he liked his sense of humor.

Frank said, "Maybe is a great nondecision.

"Look closer at the three ideas embedded in this first question: meeting the real need; informing yourself of options; and thinking it through. Start with the first: *Are you meeting the real need?*"

The young man relaxed. Perhaps it *would* help him to think more clearly if he replied either "Yes," he knew the real need for his decision, or "No," he did not.

After a moment, he answered honestly, "No."

"Fine," Frank said. "As soon as you answer 'No' to a question, you can pay more attention to it. And then you can arrive at a better decision."

The young man asked, "What do I need to pay more attention to?"

"If you answer 'No' to the first part, then you need to pay attention to where you are going.

"Most of us set out to go and get what we *want*. Usually it is because we do not know what we *need*. So we go off in the wrong direction."

The young man winced, remembering how he had gotten lost on the wrong trail that morning. "How do I know what the real need is?" he asked.

Frank said, "You can begin by asking, 'Is this something I *merely want* or what I *really need*?'"

"What's the difference?" the young man asked.

Frank replied, "A *want* is a wish.

"A *need* is a necessity.

"A want is just an attractive distraction, which we may pursue but later find unfulfilling. Even if we finally get what we've wanted, it often leaves us still wanting. A need, however, is basic and nurturing. A need is what a situation requires.

"For example, we want jam but we need bread. The jam tastes good but doesn't nourish us."

The young man exclaimed, "This is pretty basic thinking. I'll bet it's really useful for beginners."

Frank retorted, "Do I look like a beginner to you? The trouble with most people is that they forget to use the basic principles that work."

Frank paused. And then he said, "Truly success-ful people pursue first what they *need*.

"In life, we may want a fancy house but *need* a loving home. When we pursue what we want, we often miss getting what we really need. I *know*.

"If you want to be effective, do first things first. First, pursue your 'home,' then your 'house.'

"After you have done what you need to do, then, you can do what you want--but only then."

The young man thought about the difference between his business and personal needs and wants, and wondered how well he would do in the future.

He recalled examples of the short-term thinking of some Americans in the 1980s, when the Japanese had acquired a good deal of American companies and real estate. The Americans got what they wanted: big, quick profits.

But Japanese businesses got what they needed: long-term investments and assets.

The young man thought about whether he was pursuing what he wanted or what he needed.

Frank offered, "The key is focusing on the real need. Focusing means seeing a vision of only the results you really *need* and focusing on these results so clearly, and in such detail, that you can already see yourself achieving them."

The young man looked up at the blue sky and saw a sliver of pale moon. He said, "I remember seeing a tape from the early 1960s of the American president saying, 'We shall land a man on the moon and return him safely by the end of the decade.'"

Frank asked, "What made you think of that?"

"I think it is a good example of focusing on the real *need* because the president saw ahead to what was needed, including safety."

Frank nodded, "So he may have *wanted* to land men on the moon *soon*. But the real *need* was to land men on the moon and return them *safely*."

"Yes, otherwise, it might have killed the whole space program," the young man said. "And the fact that he said it would be done by the end of the decade also gave it a sense of urgency."

Frank asked, "Do you know what happened?"

"Yes. America landed men on the moon in 1969-- the end of the decade--and returned them safely. I remember seeing films of the *Apollo* capsule splashing safely into the ocean."

Frank asked, "As you recall those scenes, what do you learn about focusing on the real need?"

The young man said, "I'm beginning to see that when you focus on the real need, by saying 'No' to everything else, you get better results."

"Good," Frank said. "Do you think it would help you to focus if you wrote down, in great detail, the results that you needed, and looked at this often?"

"Yes," the young man said. So he stopped for a moment to write down the results he needed.

Then he thought more about his decision and said, "So, focusing is sensing the needed results so clearly that I don't let anything else distract me."

Frank agreed, "You focus by saying 'No' to whatever doesn't help you achieve the real need and 'Yes' only to what does."

"How can I become this decisive?"

Frank said, "Decisive people clearly know what the real need is, so they can quickly judge whether or not a specific decision will support or undermine what they need.

"Following your space example, imagine that an engineer went to his manager and proposed a way to land a man on the moon which would take at least fifteen years. What do you think a decisive manager who knew what was needed would say to that idea? 'Yes' or 'No'?"

The young man knew the answer immediately. "If your real need is to land a man on the moon and return him safely by the end of the decade, anything that would take longer than ten years would be too long. So a manager who focused on only the real need could easily say 'No.' It may be a great idea, but, 'No,' he is not going to do it."

"Exactly," Frank said. "Do you see how much easier it is to be decisive when you focus only on the real need?"

The young man said, "I'm beginning to."

"Here is another example," Frank said.

"What if an engineer went to his manager with an idea that would land a man on the moon within three years, but at great risk to the astronaut?"

The young man answered, "A focused manager would clearly say 'No' because of the risks."

Frank said, "Do you see how your decisiveness depends upon how clearly you see the real need?"

"This is very helpful," the young man said.

"The original space program knew this well," Frank continued. "No one had ever been into space, so it was important to gather whatever information they could and to use their imagination to focus on what they needed to do. It became a focused vision, and they pursued it."

The young man noted, "I've seen animated films that showed the astronauts what it was going to be like, with the capsule turning over and so forth, before they actually experienced it."

Frank said, "Sure. And the more clearly you see the results you need in the end, the easier it is to deal with whatever might happen along the way."

At that point, the two men stopped to drink from their water bottles. The young man took out his journal and wrote a reminder to himself:

*When I pursue
only the real need,*

*I am more decisive
and I make better decisions
sooner.*

"We want a lot," Frank noted, "but we need little. When we focus the decision down to only what we need--that is, what makes us feel really successful--it becomes a much easier decision.

"For example, I am a widower and do my own grocery shopping. To use a simple example, the day after my first Hike, when I went grocery shopping I tested what I had just learned by quickly asking myself, 'Do I just want this, or do I really need this?'

"I found the question worked for me.

"I came home with healthier, tastier food which I enjoyed. Now, eating better is a habit, and I feel better."

The young man asked, "How can I tell the difference between what I want and what I need?"

Frank said, "There's a practical way to do it.

"To see what you merely *want*, ask yourself, 'What do I wish I could *do*?'

"To see what you really *need,* ask, 'Looking back on this, what would I like to *have done*?'

"In the supermarket, for example, I asked, 'Later on, what would I like to have eaten?'"

The young man said, "That's helpful. I usually discover the difference between what I want and what I need when I finally get what I want and it doesn't work out as well as I'd hoped."

"Too many people in business do that," Frank said. "They do what they want rather than what is needed and harm their organizations and themselves.

"The more people I have in my organization who pursue the real need, the more we all prosper.

"Whether we are people in an organization, or individuals dealing with our own lives," Frank said, "we can each benefit from asking ourselves, *'Am I Meeting the Real Need?'*"

The young man said, "I'm beginning to see how important this is."

Then he talked about a friend who had failed as an editor at a book publishing firm. He said his friend had signed up college professors to write books which appealed only to a narrow market and resulted in few sales.

He failed because he pursued only what he wanted, *prestige*, at the expense of what he also needed, *profit*, to pay for *all* kinds of books.

Frank challenged, "Can you imagine how many decisions your friend made when he was deciding which professor should write which books? Were all those decisions of his really necessary?"

The young man realized they were not, as they did not pursue the real need: to stay in business and pay the bills, including the editor's salary, by publishing both prestigious *and* profitable books.

Then the young man realized many of his own decisions at work were probably unnecessary. He resolved to focus on his organization's real need. He could help the company and himself prosper with less wasted effort. Having worked more efficiently, he could even get home earlier.

The young man was already eliminating some of his decisions because they were not really needed. He could now concentrate on the real need for the more important decisions.

He thought about the decision he needed to make.

Frank said, "Don't get distracted by chasing the next rabbit that crosses your path. That is just something you may want to do. See what is needed and pursue the real need until you achieve it."

Frank noted, "You arrive at a better plac[
end, when you pursue the real need at the out[

Then the young man recalled what the hik[
asked at the outset of The Hike. Over lunc[
had asked themselves, "Do we want a chall[
climb, or do we need a thoughtful hike?"

He noticed they chose to take a thoughtful hike by
deciding to ascend the mountain on the gentle east-
ern slope, knowing what they needed that weekend
was quiet time to *think* about their decisions.

Frank noted, "You will soon arrive at a better
decision by asking, *'Am I Meeting the Real Need?'*"

Then the two hikers fell silent, each with his own
thoughts. Discussing the first part of the practical
question with the young man encouraged Frank to
think more about it himself. He stared off into the
distant mountain view, thinking about what he really
needed to be doing.

The men agreed to hike quietly on their own.

The young man thought about how he would
apply what he had learned.

What was the real need for his decision? If he
could do only one thing well, what did it need to be?

He thought about the decision he needed to make
and asked himself the practical question again: *"Am
I Meeting the Real Need, Informing Myself of
Options, and Thinking It Through?"*

He knew there were two more parts to the first
question, and he wondered about them.

He also knew the other hikers were asking themselves the same question.

Then the two men stopped under the shade of a
tree to rest and the young man decided to take out
his journal and write a summary of what he wanted
to remember--and to *use*:

## Meeting the Real Need: A Summary

Pursuing only the real need in the very beginning gets me better results in the end.

This means both _seeing_ a vision of needed results in such real detail that I sense myself already achieving them, & then _doing_ only what meets the real need.

Wants are wishes. Needs are necessities. Needs are essential for success and fulfillment.

To see what I merely want, I ask, "What do I want to do now?" To see what is really needed, I ask, "What would I like to _have done_?"

What do I really need from this decision? For me and for others to feel successful & fulfilled? Is my vision clearly focused on the needed results? Am I saying "Yes" to only what meets the real need, and "No" to everything else?

Am I meeting the real need?

I use my head by asking myself a practical question:

Am I Meeting the Real Need, Informing Myself of Options, and Thinking It Through?

YES___ OR NO___

# ✓ Informed Options

*Late Friday Afternoon*

Later that same afternoon, Frank introduced the young man to one of the strongest hikers in the group, Hiro Tanaka. This successful businessman owned a midsize manufacturing firm in Tokyo.

As the three men hiked together across a barren, rocky area, Frank told Hiro that the young man had asked himself the first part of the practical question.

"If I have to ask myself each part of the first question and the second question, won't it take longer to reach a decision?" the young man asked.

Frank smiled. Then he waved to Hiro and the young man as he hiked off to be on his own.

Hiro, dressed in starched khaki, spoke quietly and precisely. "What you say is true. But as we say in Japan: 'The slower I go, the sooner I arrive.'"

Then Hiro laughed and added, "The modern translation is, 'It takes less time to make a better decision than it does to correct a poor decision.'"

The young man winced as he realized from his own experience that morning how true it was.

He was beginning to realize he needed to take the time to make a better decision in the first place.

Hiro asked, "Are you ready to look at the next part of the practical question, *'Am I Meeting the Real Need, Informing Myself of Options, and Thinking It Through?'*"

The young man grinned and said, "What are my options?" Hiro laughed.

"One of the options you have," Hiro said, "is to realize that you usually do *have* options. Often there are several options, but you may not be aware of them. When you hear yourself say, 'I have no other choice,' just smile at yourself," Hiro suggested, "and know you simply are not yet *aware* of your options.

"In our fear-frozen minds we sometimes think we have no other choice. That is seldom, if ever, true. It is merely a sign of our fear that has paralyzed us."

The young man argued, "But if you don't know your options, for you, you have no options."

"When that seems to be true," Hiro said, "you need to become *aware* of the options you have."

"How do I become aware?" the young man asked.

"You can begin by asking questions and gathering needed information. 'Needed' information is only what you actually need to know to make a better decision. Anything else is extraneous information. As you gather information, do not avoid what you do not want to hear or you will not become aware of all your real options. And you will remain in illusion."

"How do I avoid that?" the young man asked.

"A good way to get all the needed information is by your own realistic observations," Hiro said.

"For example, let us say that you are in charge of finding a site for a plant nursery. You finally find a site that may be suitable if it is not too windy. You might ask the agent, who assures you that it is a sheltered location. But how can you quickly find out for yourself?"

The young man did not know, or so he thought.

Hiro asked, "What if you saw trees at the site?"

Then the young man realized, "I could look at the trees to see if any were bent from the winds."

"Exactly," Hiro said. "What can you depend more on, someone else's words or your own eyes?"

The young man remembered a time when his own observations had worked for him. He had selected his first car by looking at other cars on the road, to see what his options were.

He answered clearly, "It would be wiser for me to make my own observations."

"Yes. If you want to know more," Hiro suggested, "notice more." The young man reflected on this.

"Would it also help me to become more observant, by talking with and listening to observant people?"

"Yes," Hiro said. "Ask the most experienced people you know, those who have been down the road and back, and look for a pattern of observation and information you can rely on."

"Like talking with all of you about The Map?"

"Yes. Talk with people you feel can guide you. And listen. But be careful," he cautioned.

"Do not accept someone else's view of reality," he warned. "Validate the information yourself."

The young man said, "I'm beginning to get the message. 'Inform yourself.'"

"Yes. And if you get information from others which you know is critical to making your own decision, then verify it," Hiro suggested.

The young man thought about this and about the journey he was on. He noticed the more experienced hikers, like Hiro, were independent. They knew the route. But if he paid attention, he knew he would eventually be able to make his own way as well.

Hiro said, "You will seldom learn of your options by just sitting and waiting for them to come to you."

"Sometimes I do just that," the young man reflected. "I wonder why?"

"You may be immobilized by a subconscious fear," Hiro noted. "Fear fogs our vision.

"The worse case I know of was reflected in a very sad father's comment following the suicide of his twenty-year-old daughter. He said, 'Think of all the choices she didn't see she had.'"

Hiro was quiet for a moment as he felt the sadness the father must have known. "The saddest part is that what frightens us and paralyzes us is usually not real.

"But when you find out what *is* real by gathering information from the real world, you become more aware of the alternatives you have had all along.

"You feel better when you gather a piece of realistic information, which often leads to more information. Just by gathering information, you become less naive and more realistically informed. You begin to see more reality."

Hiro asked, "When do you think you are more apt to feel discouraged, when you feel you have options or when you don't?"

The young man said, "I feel most discouraged, of course, when I don't see that I have any options. That's the situation I'm in at work."

"Where do you think you are more apt to see your options," Hiro asked, "isolated in your own thoughts or by gathering information from the real world?"

The young man answered, "I can see that I need to get outside myself and inform myself of my options, to be more realistically aware of what is going on."

"Yes," Hiro agreed. "And you may want to remember that information is more than a collection of facts. It is also how people *feel* about the facts."

The young man paused. He realized he needed to find out more about people's feelings as well as the facts. He intended to do so in the future.

Then the young man asked, "When I gather information, that is, facts and feelings, how do I know when I have enough to make a decision?"

"There are two kinds of information," Hiro noted, "information that is nice to have, and information that you need to have.

"You may feel you never have all the information you want," Hiro said. "But ask, 'Do I have the information I need?' Remember that the needed information is only that information without which you cannot make a better decision.

"For example," Hiro said, "when we set up camp tonight, we will need to explore the terrain and make sure we have the drinking water we need nearby. Out here, an uninformed decision can be costly."

The young man stopped and made a note to himself:

✓

*As I gather more information,*
*I become more aware of my options.*

✓

"I guess I haven't been using my head and giving my options enough thought," he confided to Hiro.

"You have begun," Hiro noted, "by asking yourself, *'Am I Meeting the Real Need, Informing Myself of Options, and Thinking It Through?'*"

The young man wanted to know more and asked, "How do I discover which is my best option?"

Hiro asked, "How do *you* think you could?"

"Well, I guess I could ask myself, 'Will this option best help me to meet the real need?'"

"That's excellent," Hiro said. "You are tying this all together. Now, do you remember your first step toward arriving at a better decision?"

"Yes--to stop. When I don't know how to say 'Yes' to a better decision, I can first say 'No' to a poor decision and stop doing what doesn't work. Even if I do not know a better way, I will most likely fill this void I've created with something better."

"Exactly," Hiro said. "When you first decided to stop doing what did not work for you and to join us on The Hike, you set out to find a better way. Once you eliminated your poor option of continuing to make decisions in your old style, you increased the likelihood that you would find a better way.

"For example," Hiro continued, "last year, one of the American hikers told me that his work suffered greatly after his divorce. He thought he was still in love with his ex-wife, but she was no longer interested in him. He didn't know what to do. He could not eat. He could not sleep."

"*Was* he in love with her?"

"I do not know. But from the way he said he treated her, he did not sound very loving. Nonetheless, he believed that his only chance of being happy and productive again was to be reunited with her. Since that was not possible, he became depressed. Then something interesting happened. He became aware of his options."

"How did that happen?" the young man asked.

"He said a close friend asked him questions that helped him paint mental pictures of his real options.

"He was asked, 'When you were married, were you and your wife happy?' The man answered, 'No.' 'Do you think you and your wife have changed that much?' He answered, 'No.' Then he was asked, 'What leads you to believe you would really be happy with her if you were together now?'

"Then his friend asked him, 'Would it not be better to improve your attitude and then meet a woman who is more compatible with you?'

"His friend suggested, 'Imagine that you have learned from your past mistakes and you have corrected them. You take a sailing vacation and meet a wonderful woman who likes you. Or you meet a woman one day for a business lunch who has what you have been looking for and you date that night and discover something magical together.'

"'Or you join a bicycling club one weekend and pedal next to an interesting lady whom you meet later for a game of bridge and with whom you develop a nurturing, enjoyable relationship.'

"'Or imagine. . .'" Hiro said as he left the next possibility open to the young man's imagination.

The young man smiled and said, "I'll bet before long he felt a lot better."

Hiro said, "Certainly, because it was more realistic. When he stopped feeling sorry for himself and saw the reality of other possibilities, he realized he could develop a variety of options. It was up to him. The reality was that these and other options were always there. He just was not aware of them."

The young man thought about the decision he needed to make. He noted, "So the problem is not that we *have* no options, but that we are not *aware* of the options we have. We just don't see them yet.

"How could the divorced man have seen his options earlier?" the young man wanted to know.

Hiro responded, "How do *you* think he could have become aware of his options?"

"Well, I can become aware of my options by personally gathering needed information, so I guess he could do the same--get more information."

"Yes," Hiro said. "So, how would he discover his options by gathering information?"

"I suppose," the young man said, "he could find out if there were bicycling clubs nearby, or video dating services, or . . ."

"Yes," Hiro noted. "He could gather information, even if he didn't want to. He needed to know more. Now what do you think about your saying 'Sometimes there is just no other choice'?"

"I didn't realize that so many options were usually there," the young man said, "or that getting information would help me see more of my options."

Then the young man said, "I've just remembered a story about Henry Ford and the importance about getting information before making a decision.

"After he took three regional managers to dinner, he soon chose one man to be his national manager.

"When the man later asked him why he had been chosen, Ford replied, 'You had all been successful at selling, but you were the only one who tasted his food before he salted it. I like a manager who gets information before making his decision.'"

The young man smiled as he realized he didn't always get the information he needed to know before he made his decisions. He wondered what opportunities he'd missed. With that in mind, he thanked Hiro. And then he went off by himself to think.

Later he sat on a tree stump and quietly wrote several insights and questions in his journal:

# Informing Myself of Options: A Summary

First, I realize I probably have several options I am not _aware_ of.

As I gather the needed information, I become more aware of my options.

I choose the option which meets the real need.

_Information_ is a collection of facts and feelings: that is, what really is, & how people feel about it.

I gather the needed information. I observe it, or if someone gives me the information, I verify it.

Do I have the information I need? Who has it? Where is it? What is the best way to get it? Have I verified it myself?

As I gather the needed information, what do I see my options are? Am I Informing Myself of Options?

I use my head by asking myself a practical question:

Am I Meeting the Real Need, Informing Myself of Options, and Thinking It Through?

YES ___ OR NO ___

## √
## *Thinking It Through*

T hat night, after resting and enjoying the view at sunset, the group hiked along slowly, led by the guide, who encouraged them to experience what it was like to try to find their way in the dark.

"This is how we often make decisions--in the dark," the guide said. "We could light our way by asking ourselves a couple of questions, but we stay in the dark when we forget to ask."

After an hour of slow progress, the thoughtful hikers doubled back to where they had last spotted a stream and they camped for the night.

The young man shivered in his thin jacket as he helped start the campfire. He wished he had anticipated the cold on the upper mountain. He should have known better. He just hadn't thought ahead. He rubbed his hands together to stay warm.

Noticing this, Ingrid Bauer, a brilliant woman who headed a growing international consulting firm, offered him her extra sweater. She smiled and said, "It's a good thing I like to wear my sweaters large." He accepted gratefully.

"I've heard from Frank that you wish you had a mentor, an older person at work to guide you."

"That's right." The young man laughed. "You don't happen to know of one in my town, do you?"

She smiled. "No, I don't. But I can understand why you would want one," she said. "In Germany, we have the guild system, in which young people work under a master for many years before they are qualified for a position. The training is excellent. I know guilds are not available here, so people need to have their own system of training.

"It may be useful," Ingrid noted, "for you to realize you already have an older mentor. *You*!

"You," she added, "are your own older mentor. As an older and hopefully wiser person, you can examine your past decisions and your results. Looking closely at your previous decisions will teach you more than you can learn from anyone else.

"You can learn what not to do from your poor results and what to do from your better results."

The young man remembered the results of some of his poor decisions, and his face showed it.

Ingrid turned up the flame on the portable lantern next to her and said, "Lighten up. Don't be so hard on yourself." The young man smiled.

"Just look at your past results and let *them* enlighten you. Your results are your best teachers.

"Where are you now on The Map?" she asked.

"So far, I have asked myself the first two parts of the practical question, *'Am I Meeting the Real Need, Informing Myself of Options, and Thinking It Through?'*"

Ingrid asked, "Would you like to look at the third part, *'Am I Thinking It Through?'*"

The young man said, "Yes."

He thought about his own decision and quickly realized he hadn't really thought it through. He was quiet.

Ingrid asked, "Do you remember your telling us at lunch about the guide jumping out of harm's way from the poisonous snake on the trail?"

"Yes, and in seconds. How did he do that?"

"The guide had thought it through," Ingrid said. "Before he began The Hike, he had already asked himself, 'If a snake struck out from the underbrush, or if rocks fell from above, or if a ledge gave way, then what would happen? Then what?'

"The guide had already looked ahead at where he needed to be. We can learn to do it too. What we think through, we can be ready for.

"For example, a good chess player thinks several moves ahead in order to win."

"How can we learn to do that?" he asked.

"We can imagine any situation we might find ourselves in and simply ask, *Then what would probably happen? Then what? Then what?*' until we think the situation through."

Ingrid said, "As we 'hike' through business and life, we need to watch for danger and be alert."

The young man realized, "So the rocks and snakes will be there, but if we anticipate them and think things through, we can still do well."

"Yes," Ingrid said. "I find that asking myself, *'Then what?' 'Then what?'* really helps me to think things through and to get the results I need."

The young man said, "So before I make my decision, it could be useful to take each of my options and ask, 'Then what would happen? Then what?'"

"Yes. Imagine, in detail, what would eventually happen if you acted upon your tentative decision."

They sat in silence while the young man asked himself, "If I were to proceed with my initial decision, what would probably happen? Then what?" He soon realized he would not get the needed results.

He knew he needed to make a better decision.

The young man then thought through a different option, and when he did, it seemed more likely to get him the better results he needed.

Ingrid commented, "I have seen many clients who have suffered major business setbacks just because they did not think through their decisions."

"Can you give me an example?" he asked.

"Certainly," Ingrid responded. "Would you like a corporate example or an individual example?"

"Both, please," the young man requested.

"The American automobile industry declined when oil prices rose and people became more aware of their environment. Too many executives did not think their decisions through. Their goal was to make money, and they made more on larger automobiles. So when the demand for smaller cars came along, they made poor-quality small cars, assuming that unsatisfied customers would return to their old habits of buying larger cars.

"But they did not anticipate something.

"The executives did not ask, 'If we do not provide what the market demands, then what will probably happen? Then what? Then what?'

"Because they did not think it through, they left the door open for other manufacturers to establish a foothold by producing high-quality small cars. Enter foreign automobile manufacturers.

"As the public discovered which manufacturers met their needs, some buyers switched their allegiance and many never returned to American cars.

"As time went on, these other manufacturers strengthened their dealerships and their image and eventually even established their own plants in this country. With so much infrastructure in place, they became a powerful force in the industry.

"The American companies' market share fell and it cost many workers their jobs.

"If their managers had thought it through, they would have seen the ongoing need for high-quality small cars and they could have met the demand.

"Now, the wiser ones are doing just that, but they have a lot of catching up to do."

The young man said, "That is also a good example of it taking less time to stop and ask yourself the questions you need to help you make a better decision than it does to correct a poor decision later on."

"Yes," Ingrid said. "And that is also why it is so important to have enough people in an organization asking themselves such questions before making decisions that can affect the whole organization."

He thought to himself, "If this System really works as well as she says, maybe I'll introduce it to my company."

"To give you an individual example," Ingrid continued, "we once needed to hire someone new to head up our Paris office. When I returned from my first Hike three years ago, my senior partners had someone they wanted to hire. We all took the candidate out to lunch, but as I interviewed her, I wondered if she really was the right person.

"Later, after speaking with my partners and encouraging them to ask themselves the two questions which I learned to ask myself on The Hike, they realized they had almost made a costly mistake.

"They realized that they had not really thought their decision through. They had reservations about the candidate but had not wanted to admit them, even to themselves. They were fooling themselves.

"They just wanted to fill the position quickly. But when they asked, *'Then what would probably happen? Then what?'* they saw they would probably just have to replace her in six months.

"So, we focused on the real need and developed our options by seeing other candidates, and eventually hired a superb person.

"The person heading our Paris office has been contributing to our spectacular growth ever since. We shudder when we think of what we almost did.

"Ever since then, we have encouraged each other to each think through our decisions and it has rewarded us well.

"In fact, all our associates now use the 'Yes' or 'No' System of making better decisions as a basic part of our doing business."

The young man made a note in his journal:

✓

To make a better decision,

I ask, "Then what
would probably happen?
Then what...?  Then what...?"

Until I think my decision
through to a better result.

✓

The young man realized that the simple idea of asking, "Then what?" could be invaluable to him.

He looked up from the campfire and saw storm clouds. He noticed others collecting wood for the next morning's breakfast fire and covering the dry wood with canvas to protect it from possible rain during the night. He knew they were thinking ahead and anticipating what might happen.

Preparing the wood in advance was a small thing, but he realized that it might make a big difference to all of them at breakfast the next morning. He asked himself, "What can I think through now to help me get better results later on?"

Ingrid said, "Remember, as Hiro says, 'Better results are like butterflies. If you chase them, you can exhaust yourself and the results may escape you.'"

The young man asked, "But how do you get better results if you don't go after them?"

"Focus on the real need, inform yourself of your options, and think each option through. Then let the better results come more easily to you."

The young man thought again about his own decision. He began to believe that he just might get better results if he used this System.

"Who decides what 'better results' are?" he asked Ingrid.

"You do," she said. "To begin with, you decide what your real need is. And you measure the results you get by how well *your* results satisfy *your* need.

"That is why it is so important for you to be clear about the real need from the beginning and to develop your options and to think it through."

The young man thought about how much more he was now using his head to make his own decision.

Then Ingrid asked, "Have you ever been disappointed with one of your better decisions?"

"Not with one of my *better* decisions," the young man said.

"Think about it," she suggested. "Have you ever regretted something about your better decisions?"

"The only regret I've ever had about making a better decision is that I didn't make it sooner."

"Exactly! And why didn't you make it sooner?"

He said, "I guess because I didn't think of it."

"And why didn't you think of it?"

"I guess I just didn't give it enough thought at the time," the young man admitted.

Ingrid was quiet.

The young man thought. Then he realized, "So, that's why it is well worth taking the time to ask myself valuable questions! The questions stimulate me to think more about my decision and they lead to my making a better decision *sooner*!"

The young man had been too concerned about the time he lost asking himself questions in order to find his answers. But he understood now what Hiro had said about investing the time. It would help him reach a better decision *sooner*. It would save time!

The young man asked Ingrid, "Why don't we take the time to think things through?"

"When we don't think our decisions through," Ingrid offered, "it may be because we assume it is only a short-term decision--but often it is not.

"Our lives are shaped by decisions which we do not think are all that important at the time. But our decisions work like dominoes.

"The results of one decision can affect the next decision--more than we realize--and we need to respect this.

"After you think about your decision and ask yourself, *'Have I really thought it through?'*" she said, "you may want to sleep on it. Then you may want to review it again tomorrow morning."

The young man decided to spend the rest of the evening alone. He thanked Ingrid, and left.

As he sipped a mug of hot chocolate outside his tent, he wrote his observations in his journal. He planned to review his notes again in the morning.

Later, however, he was awakened by the sound of heavy rain on his tent. As he lay in his warm sleeping bag, he mulled over the specific decision he was making. Then he turned on a flashlight and read his notes:

# Thinking It Through: A Summary

My past decisions are my own best mentors. Looking at them realistically can teach me more than any person to avoid illusion and see reality.

As I look at my results, I am not too hard on myself. I lighten up. I did the best I knew how.

Now I get better results because I focus on meeting the real need, informing myself of options, and thinking things through to a better result.

To see how good my results are, I measure them against my meeting the real need.

What would the results have to be to fill the real need? If I act on my decision, What would probably happen? Then what? ... Then what? What do I fear would be the worst result? What would the best result be? What would I do in the worst/best case? How clearly do I foresee the most likely results? For me? For others? Have I Thought It Through?

I use my head by asking myself a practical question:

Am I Meeting the Real Need, Informing Myself of Options, and Thinking It Through?

YES___ OR NO___

√

## *The Other Half*

Early Saturday morning, just before daylight, the young man joined the guide for breakfast. The storm had cleared overnight, but since the ground was still wet, they both stood up around the fire.

The guide sipped his hot coffee and watched oatmeal being cooked over the open flames. He asked, "Well, has the first half of the 'Yes' or 'No' System helped you to make a better decision yet?"

Since he had begun The Hike, the young man had been asking himself, *"Am I Meeting the Real Need, Informing Myself of Options, and Thinking It Through?"*

He answered slowly, "Using my head by asking myself the first of the two questions has already helped me to make a better decision.

"So why do I need the next half of the System?"

The guide responded, "To make a far better decision. When most of us make a decision, we do only one of two important things: we either use our heads or we listen to our hearts.

"But we seldom do both. So we often make half-decisions based on half-truths.

"Notice that we have hiked only halfway up this mountain. The second half of both the mountain and the System can be more difficult, but it is also more rewarding."

The young man said, "I want to know more about that, but there's something I'd like to know first.

"Before going on to the second half, I'd like to understand the basis for the whole system. Why does asking myself questions help me so much?"

"Because questions propel us to find answers. We often make poor decisions because we did not first ask ourselves a few simple questions."

The young man was bothered by the word "simple." As young as he was, he had already become skeptical of simplistic answers. He had tried them before and found they just hadn't worked.

The guide seemed to read his thoughts. "As you come to discover the extraordinary power of the simple," he warned the young man, "beware of the simplistic."

The young man admitted, "I'm not sure I know the difference between simple and simplistic."

"Simplistic," the guide cautioned, "is less than what is needed. A simplistic answer is an illusion.

"But simple is all that is needed and nothing more.

"That is why the better answers, the ones that more easily get better results, are invariably simple. Sometimes they are the most difficult ones to see.

"But once you discover the simple answer, it becomes the obvious answer. Making a better decision often depends on seeing, at the time, what becomes obvious to you later."

The young man asked, "Can you give me an example?"

"Yes. Making a poor investment is an example. People who have lost money on an investment often look back and say, 'If only I had taken the time to ask more questions.'"

The guide then challenged, "Why do you think it is that we do not ask questions more often?"

"I guess because we don't always know what to ask," the young man answered. "Or we really don't want to ask. We want to be given the answers without taking the time to ask the questions."

The young man thought about Socrates, the great teacher in ancient Greece who helped students find their own answers by asking questions. He recalled that this method had been used for centuries.

"Questions are like alarm clocks," the guide noted. "Questions wake us up."

"Wake us up to what?" the young man asked.

"To reality--to what is really going on *around* us and *within* us," the guide replied.

"Every effective decision we have ever made," he noted, "has been based on reality. Unfortunately, we have all made both kinds of decisions: effective ones and ineffective ones."

"What's the real difference," the young man asked, "between effective and ineffective decisions?"

The guide said, "Our ineffective decisions are based on *illusions* we believe at the time. Our effective decisions are built on *realities* we recognize. That is why it is useful to ask ourselves probing questions to help us distinguish illusion from reality.

"The questions shine a light on the illusion."

"What do you mean by illusion?"

"An illusion is a fiction we believe because we want to--even though it turns out to be false.

"Making a decision based upon a fiction we believe," the guide offered, "is like building a beautiful house on a foundation of loose sand. It is only a matter of time until the house collapses. In the meantime, the person feels an uneasiness, though he may push it back to the darkest corner of his mind.

"To live in an illusion is to live with a constant dull pain. We know something is wrong but we do not want to know what it is. We deny it and hope it will go away, but it doesn't.

"It is like a chronic headache we once knew was painful but we eventually accept and become accustomed to. We accept the dull pain as tolerable. But the illusion, like the pain, drains us whether we are aware of it or not."

The young man realized that was how he had felt lately. "So, what's missing?" he asked.

"Your own feelings are missing," the guide said. "Perhaps you would like to see where we are going in the second half." He turned and walked with the young man at his side for half a mile, crossing a creaking, swaying wooden bridge that spanned a gap separating where they had camped from the higher part of the mountain they would ascend today.

They walked another two hundred yards beyond the bridge to the edge of a shallow pond. The guide said, "Look into the pool and tell me what you see."

The young man leaned over the water and looked down through the dawn's faint light into the still pool. "I see rocks at the bottom."

"Change your focus. Now, what do you see?"

"I see myself," the young man replied, "or at least my reflection."

The guide said, "Now, you can see the important part that is missing from your decision: it is you. *You* are missing from your own decision.

"Like all of us, you make your decisions based on your character--with what is in your heart--whether you realize it or not. You need to cross back and forth across the bridge between the two halves of yourself--the thinking half in your head, and the feeling half in your heart--if you want to consistently make better decisions.

"The bridge is just your awareness that you need to connect these two halves of yourself.

"And you can learn to do this soon. Just ask yourself the private question you will learn. Then, after you have looked into the privacy of your heart, ask yourself the practical question again. When you do, you will likely arrive at a far better decision."

The guide went on to say, "More often than we realize, the way to quickly arrive at better results is to get around the obstacle that is in our way. It is usually our obstructive *self*."

"So how do we get around ourselves?" the young man wanted to know.

The guide answered, "With our character."

"What do you mean by 'our character'?" the young man asked.

"Our character," the guide noted, "is our collection of personal beliefs and how we act on them.

"How we make our decisions depends mostly on what we believe. Our beliefs are often forgotten choices we made long ago. But they are still influential, through our subconscious, upon our decisions."

Noticing the young man's glance to the ground, the guide realized his discomfort. "Beliefs are a private matter," the guide said, "so you may not want to share your beliefs with everyone. But you may need to examine them more closely for yourself."

"What do my personal beliefs have to do with my practical decisions?" the young man asked.

The guide said, "You will use only those parts of your character that you believe have real value for you. And that may affect your decision greatly.

"Your practical decisions are mirrors of your personal thoughts, feelings, and beliefs on display for everyone to see. They clearly reveal the way you view the world and yourself.

"You can see another person's beliefs just by looking at enough of his or her decisions. Just as any aware person can see your beliefs by looking at the pattern of your past decisions."

The young man did not like the idea that his beliefs could be seen so easily by others, but he sensed the truth of it.

He made a note to himself:

✓

*My decisions reveal my beliefs.*

✓

The guide said, "You remember we spoke about there being two questions.

"You have asked yourself the practical 'head question' about *your situation.* Now you may want to ask yourself the private second question--a 'heart question' about *yourself,* the decision maker."

"A question about me?" the young man asked.

"Yes. The private question concerns your personal beliefs about: (1) your integrity, (2) your intuition, and (3) your insight into your own worth."

"What are we going to look at me for?" the young man asked, somewhat defensively.

"*We* are not going to look at you. *You* are.

"Looking closely at our own character makes many of us uncomfortable," the guide recognized. "But don't worry, you will find it most helpful."

"Why?" the young man asked.

"Because the more aware you are of your own character, the more often you make better decisions."

The young man pondered this and realized, "So, as the practical question wakes me up to my situation, the private question wakes me up to my character."

"Hopefully," the guide said with a smile. "When you knowingly apply your character to your situation, you make a better decision."

The guide suggested, "Let's continue this conversation over a hot breakfast."

They returned to the campfire to ward off the early morning chill with hot cereal and toast.

Noticing their return, the other hikers asked to join the young man and the guide in their discussion. When asked, the young man said he was just beginning to think about how important it was for him to look at his beliefs.

Hiro offered, "When we were hiking in the dark last night, it occurred to me that--as we may light a lamp and carry it out in front of us to light our way-- in a similar way, our beliefs are the lights that lead us to the decisions we make. The problem is, we are not aware of the beliefs we are carrying."

The young man said, "Sometimes I think I make *most* of my decisions in the dark."

The group laughed and the guide said, "I notice you can laugh at your own folly. That's good. The more we lighten up, as we examine our decisions, the sooner we arrive at a better decision. Who said, 'He who travels lightest travels farthest'?"

The young man suggested, "It was probably some clever ancient Oriental sage." Hiro laughed.

Ingrid smiled and said, "No doubt. Like most wisdom, what we are discovering is really not new. It was discovered by others thousands of years ago. It is not even always new to us. We just forget to use what we have known works. Let's face it, we have returned to The Hike just to remind ourselves."

Frank asked the young man, "Still think this is for beginners? Earlier, you told me, young man, that you wanted someday to be the president of a company, maybe even the one you work for now.

"If so, remember that when a CEO looks to hire a president, he doesn't say, 'What I want is a hard-driving, savvy person who knows the product.' He looks for the valuable essentials in a man."

The young man asked, "What does he look for?"

"A smart CEO asks, 'Does this person have the kind of character it takes to get the job done?'"

"Why do you look for character?" the young man wanted to know.

Frank, a CEO himself, explained, "Because, more often than not, a person with character will make better decisions, especially a person with integrity, intuition, and insight."

"Why those three traits?" the young man asked.

Frank replied, "*Integrity*, because people who have integrity won't fool themselves about a situation. They will cut through the nonsense and get to the true core of things quickly.

"*Intuition*, because people who have learned to trust their intuition won't look to others to make their tough decisions. They can depend on themselves and the CEO, in turn, can depend on them.

"And *insight*, because if people are unaware that they can unknowingly sabotage their own results, my company will eventually pay the price for it.

"When you find top people with these character traits, you hire them and pay them well, because they will pay for themselves many times over."

The young man smiled and said, "I think I want to get on to the private question about character."

The group laughed. Frank came straight to the point. "The private question you can ask yourself is *'Does My Decision Show I Am Honest with Myself, Trust My Intuition, and Deserve Better?'*"

The young man was surprised. He began to think about what he had heard and realized it was going to take a good deal more thought.

Then the guide smiled and said, "With that in mind, let's all help break camp and ascend to the summit."

√
# My Integrity

Later that morning, the young man spotted Angela Cuvero, a personable Brazilian teenager, resting near the stream during the morning hiking break. She was with her father, Santo Cuvero, a prominent industrialist.

He greeted them both and said to her, "Angela, I noticed several people asking you questions during this hike. May I ask you why?"

She laughed. "That's because last year I was on my first Hike and was having some problems. They wanted to know if I used The Map to arrive at better decisions this year and if it worked."

"And. . .?" the young man inquired.

She smiled. "I did, and it did. I used The Map a lot and it really helped me."

"What difficulties were you having?" he asked.

"I had some troubles," Angela said, "but you don't need to hear about that." She no longer needed to romance her problems for attention. She was now more interested in finding answers.

He admitted, "I know what you mean about having troubles. I haven't told this to anyone, but I'm having problems at work and at home. But there doesn't seem to be much I can do about it."

"Just who do you think you're kidding?" the young woman asked abruptly.

He was startled. He didn't know what to say.

Then she laughed, "I've been wanting to say that to someone for almost a year now. That's what they said to me last year."

He claimed, "I'm not trying to kid anybody."

The young woman asked, "Aren't you? Aren't you trying to kid somebody?"

The young man knew that Angela thought he was kidding himself but he didn't like the idea. He asked, "How would you know?"

"I've been there," Angela said. "I've learned that the reason most of us have problems is that we fool ourselves."

"What happened last year?" he asked.

"They talked to me about 'truth,' 'reality,' 'integrity,' and 'honesty.' But I just got confused. Finally they helped me figure it out for myself."

The young man admitted, "I wouldn't mind having a more practical understanding of all those things myself."

She said, "Well, the way I use what I've learned is simple and it works for me in my everyday life. 'Reality' is whatever really is. 'Truth' is a description of reality--mine or somebody else's.

"'Integrity' is telling myself the truth. And 'honesty' is telling the truth to other people.

"I put this all together now," she said, "by looking at what I really think and do. And then I look at what really happens to me. I look at my choices and the real consequences. It's helped me not to fool myself or lie to others as much.

"And before long, things started getting better for me."

Then Angela laughed. "Surprise! Surprise! It's amazing how much easier everything has become all of a sudden. It must be a coincidence."

The young man laughed. "So, how did you learn last year to really tell yourself the truth?"

"The others encouraged me to just keep using the private question on The Map, *'Does My Decision Show I Am Honest with Myself, Trust My Intuition, and Deserve Better?'*

"They especially encouraged me to concentrate on the first part, *'Am I Honest with Myself?'*

"Even if I didn't think it was working, they encouraged me to just keep asking the question over and over again. It was just repetition."

The young man thought about what she had said.

"Then," she said, "to help me see how common it was for people to avoid telling themselves the truth, several adults told me that they realized almost too late that they were often fooling themselves."

"Did that surprise you?" the young man said.

"Well, yes. When I was in trouble, adults were always telling me to stop kidding myself. So I thought they usually told themselves the truth."

The young man said, "Maybe they wanted you to learn from their mistakes."

"I guess so. It seems a lot of us are afraid of the truth. We believe if we hide from the truth we are safer, or at least more comfortable."

He admitted, "But we don't feel safer, do we?"

"No," the young woman agreed. "When we have to hide from the truth, we feel more frightened.

"For some strange reason," she said, looking straight at him, "you seem to be afraid of the truth."

"How would *you* know?" he retorted.

Angela laughed. "As I said, I have been where you are. I became angry when someone tried to tell me the truth and I didn't want to hear it. Especially if it was from my parents.

"I felt threatened and would strike out at them. I've learned now that my anger just shows my fear."

She said, "I didn't know that integrity, telling myself the truth, was really nurturing for me. I thought it was just something I was *supposed* to do."

The young man said, "And we don't want to do what we are supposed to do, do we? We do what we want to do."

"That's right," the teenager said. "Then I started to look at what I secretly wanted to do, and I asked myself, 'Would I like to have my friends and family read about this in the newspaper?'"

Overhearing them, the guide and the other hikers asked to join in on the conversation. Angela and the young man readily agreed.

The young man admitted, "I guess I'm not always as honest with the people I work with as I would like to think. Or even with my family."

Ingrid said, "I've learned that once I tell myself the truth, it is easier for me to be honest with others."

"How do you *find* the truth?" he asked her.

Ingrid said, "I find the quickest way for me to find the truth is to look for the fiction I believe--the untruth I want to believe is truth--because it is more convenient or more comfortable for me to believe it.

"The fiction is sometimes more glaring and thus easier for me to see than the truth. Once I see the fiction, I look for the opposite and find the truth."

Angela said, "I do that too. It's like that television ad for motor oil that showed a garage mechanic with a can of oil, saying, 'You can pay me a little money now.' Then the ad showed the mechanic removing the car's engine and saying, 'Or you can pay me a lot more money later.'"

The young man said, "So, in your example, the fiction is you can get away with not spending the time or money to put oil in your car, and it will still all work out just fine. But the reality is that your engine will eventually burn out."

The young man then realized aloud, "So the truth is the opposite of the fiction. If I want the engine to run well, I must add motor oil to it, like it or not."

Frank injected, "Yes. And it doesn't matter if you believe you need to add oil or not. Reality is still reality, regardless of your belief in your illusion."

Hiro added, "It is like the people who believed long ago that the Earth was flat. The Earth was round, regardless of what the people believed. Believing it was flat did not make it flat."

The young man said, "So, our believing in an illusion doesn't make it true. And believing our own illusions can just make matters worse.

"So the basis for all my better decisions is my seeing the truth and my being honest with myself."

Everyone in the group smiled, and some broke out in applause. Angela was grinning.

The young man was embarrassed, but then he smiled and continued. "The guide spoke earlier about our poor decisions being based on our illusions. I must admit that when I look back on a poor decision, I can see sometimes where I just fooled myself.

"But how can I recognize the illusion at the time?"

Ingrid responded, "If you asked the people who cared about you, might they see your illusion?"

"Other people usually see our mistakes more easily than we do," the young man acknowledged.

"Yes," she said, "and often you can see theirs. So, if you are blind to your illusion, who might be able to help you see it?"

"The people who care about me?"

"Yes," Angela said. She volunteered, "Last year, I went home and asked my friends what they saw." She laughed. "And, boy, did they tell me! They all told me, in various ways, the same things. When I saw what they saw, I made some changes."

He wanted to know what they saw, but Frank challenged the young man, "What part of you holds on to an illusion you believe?"

The young man guessed, "My ego?"

They were all silent.

Then the young man laughed. He was beginning to see their style. When they were quiet, they were giving him a chance to think for himself.

He said knowingly, "My ego holds on to my illusions."

"Good," Frank said. "Knowing that it's your ego that hangs on to your illusions, how could you make better--that is, more realistic--decisions?"

"I could put my ego aside for the moment," he said. "Then I could ask others what they saw."

"And how would you know if what others saw was true for you?"

The young man answered, "First, I would really listen to them. Then, I would see if what they said fit with my experience. Later, I would see how their insights could help me see the truth on my own."

"If you do that," Frank said, "you will do well."

"Can you give me a business example of using this?" the young man asked.

"Would you like an American example or a European one?" Ingrid offered.

"I'll take an American example."

She responded, "For years, a pioneering company thought that because they had once made the best photocopying machines, they still did. But they were losing more and more of their market share.

"When the company's wise CEO made their engineers do a side-by-side test with other copiers, they 'discovered' the competition had better-quality copying machines that cost less."

"What did the American company do?" he asked.

"As soon as they saw the truth, they went to work on reengineering their machines to give their customers the high quality they needed."

"Now, I remember," the young man recalled. "The people in that company went on to win the Baldrige Award for the best-quality organization."

"Yes, they did," Ingrid acknowledged. "And more important for their bottom line, they made more sales and gained a greater market share. The company became financially healthier and the employees' jobs became that much more secure.

"Like them, our challenge is to discover the truth. Once we see the truth, our decision is clear. It becomes obvious."

"The more we see reality," Frank said, "the more apt we are to make better decisions."

"Could you give me an example of this outside of business?" the young man asked.

Angela's father, Santo Cuvero, answered. "Yes. But as an American, you may not be comfortable with this example any more than those people who preferred to believe the illusion at the time.

"In the 1980s many Americans felt optimistic about their country, themselves, and their economy at a time when they were going further and further into debt and selling off many valuable assets to pay for this sense of well-being. It was like burning down the house to keep warm.

"Before the Americans realized the significance of this," Santo continued, "much of their business and real estate was sold to people in other countries. Eventually they lost control over more and more of what had once been their own."

The young man asked, "How could people be feeling better and doing poorly at the same time?"

"After a recession, the people's leaders helped them feel good," Santo responded. "They sold the idea of national prosperity, and people wanted to believe the illusion. So they did.

"However, the economic reality was that America went from being the largest creditor nation to the biggest debtor nation. And amazingly enough, it all happened in less than one decade.

"It wasn't only in America that this happened. People in other countries fell into similar traps.

"Leaders in the former Soviet Union believed they could afford to spend huge sums of money on sophisticated technology, instead of providing food for their own people. Now it has come to light that their economy, indeed their whole social structure, collapsed under the weight of this expensive illusion.

"Whether we see it or not, the consequences of believing an illusion eventually make things more difficult. The American people and the Soviet people may recover, just as you and I may recover from periods in our personal lives when we have lived in illusion. But they will pay an economic price for it."

The young man spoke of the troubles in American financial institutions in the late 1980's and early 1990's. "I have read that if the basic problems had been faced when they were first seen, remedying them would have cost a fraction of what it later cost. I understand that waiting a full ten years to face the truth cost the taxpayer more than ten times as much.

"Why did they delay their decisions?" he asked.

One of the American hikers said, "*They?* We may not like to see this, but *we* are the public. We chose the illusion, the paint job over the house of termites. Our officials reflect *our* expectations.

"We are the people and our elected officials our representatives. We each need to learn to make better decisions sooner or we will collectively pay a high price. We can't wait for our 'leaders.'"

"And time is of the essence," Frank said.

"*When* we make our decision is as important as what we decide to do. In this day and age, we all need to make better decisions *sooner.*"

Hiro agreed. "For example, when we hike with the guide and come upon an ice bridge, he makes it clear that if we wait, the sun could warm the ice, weaken the bridge, and endanger our crossing. We need to act soon, not wait until the situation is worse.

"The truth is, the sun is going to melt the ice, whether we see the truth of this or not. Our perception doesn't affect the reality.

"We need to look at whatever 'the melting ice' is in our own decision and deal with it soon."

Someone laughed. "When we live in illusion, we look to others like an ostrich that buries its head in the sand. We think if we cover our eyes and don't see the truth, then it won't be there.

"While we ignore the sun overhead, the once-solid ice bridge melts out from under us."

Angela Cuvero said, "On last year's hike, a person showed me something that has helped me to understand this ever since.

"I wrote it down to remind myself of it."

Angela took a piece of paper from her wallet and handed it to the young man. It read:

✓

*The sooner I see the truth,*
*the sooner I make a better decision.*

✓

The young man handed the paper back to Angela and then made a note in his journal. He realized now that the purpose of asking himself the "Yes" or "No" questions was to help him discover the truth.

One of the other hikers said, "We need to ask ourselves, 'Are we going to look for the truth or hide from it?'"

Frank said, "Let's face it, whether it is convenient or not and whether we agree with it or not, the basis of all of our better decisions are the actions we take based on the *truth*. Because, sooner or later, everything else falls apart on us."

The young man said, "I remember an important thought from a book by Buckminster Fuller. He said, *'Integrity is the essence of everything successful.'*"

As he said it, the young man realized he needed to apply what he had read. He needed to look for, and rely on, the truth more often than he had in the past.

When the conversation finished, the young man thought of more questions he could ask himself to help him see the truth.

He spent the remainder of Saturday morning hiking with the group, enjoying the scenery, and thinking about what he needed to remember.

Later, he reviewed what he had learned about his own integrity and summarized it in his journal:

# My Integrity: A Summary

My poor decisions were based on illusions I believed at the time. My better decisions are based on realities I recognize in time.

The sooner I see the truth, the sooner I make a better decision. To find the truth, I look for it.

The better decision is based on the simple answer as it eventually becomes the obvious answer.

To discover the truth, I look for the fiction I want to believe is true but cannot really count on.

We see each other's mistakes more easily, so I often park my ego & ask others what they can see and then I notice what really feels true to me.

Have I looked closely enough at my past decisions to learn from them? Have I done a reality check by observing what is really going on around me and within me? Have I noticed the obvious? Do I see the truth? Am I Telling Myself The Truth?

I consult my heart by asking myself a private question:

Does My Decision Show I Am Honest with Myself, Trust My Intuition, and Deserve Better?

YES ___ OR NO ___

√

## *My Intuition*
---

At Saturday's lunch, the young man sought out Peter Golden, a young, ingenious advertising executive whose peaceful composure suggested he knew something quite valuable. He found the wiry, bespectacled man eating alone, sitting atop a large boulder as he looked out over a gorge.

Peter turned and extended an invitation to join him. "So, you are up here looking at your decisions. Have you started to use The Map?"

"Yes. I am using it for a decision I need to make. So far I have asked myself the practical question and I have asked the first part of the private question."

As they ate, Peter asked, "Would it help you to ask yourself *'Am I Trusting My Intuition?'*"

The young man immediately thought about his decision and began to look at how he felt about it.

Peter said, "It may help you to ask yourself, 'How do I feel about *how* I am making this decision?'"

The young man had not thought so much about how he felt about *how* he made a decision as much as how he felt about the decision he had reached.

"What do you mean by how I feel about how I make my decision? Feel in what way?"

Peter suggested, "Ask yourself, for example, 'Do I feel calm or anxious?' 'Paralyzed or confident?' 'Drained or energized?'

"If the way you feel about how you are making your decision doesn't feel right to you, you probably need to change your decision to a better one.

"When you make your decision," he continued, "ask yourself if you're relying on others' opinions, or relying on your own feelings--your intuition--or, better yet, on your *better* intuition?"

"I'm not sure what you mean by my intuition, let alone my *better intuition*," the young man admitted.

Peter said, "Let's begin with your intuition and then we can get to your *better* intuition.

"Your own intuition is your own unconscious knowledge based on your own personal experiences. It's what *you* somehow sense is right for *you*."

"What do you mean by 'what I sense' is right?"

"When you are making a specific decision, like the one you are working on now, what do you sense? Do you feel a sense of calm or stress? A sense of effort or of ease? Do you feel afraid or enthusiastic?

"In short, how do you feel as you are making this decision? And what does how you feel about it tell you about its most likely outcome?"

The young man admitted, "I'm afraid my intuition or my ability to predict outcome isn't very good."

"Perhaps it is better than you realize and you just need to develop your intuition," Peter said. "It may take some time to learn, but it's absolutely invaluable, both in business and in one's personal life."

"How do I develop my intuition?" the young man wanted to know.

"You can begin," Peter suggested, "by looking back at how you made your past decisions. Recall what you *sensed* at the time you were making a specific decision. Then look at the *consequences*.

"You can relate what you sensed then to the results you got later and see how they connect. By personal observation you can teach yourself how your feelings at the time may forecast your results.

"When you have felt poorly as you were making a decision," Peter said, "for example, like making it anxiously, what were your results usually like?"

"Usually poor," the young man remembered.

"I have had the same experience," Peter said. "If I feel poorly about how I have made the decision, the results are often poor as well.

"To use your intuition, it is important to look at how you feel as you are making your decision.

"If you make it feeling a lot of effort, you are probably trying to force things to happen. If so, it will probably turn out poorly for you.

"If, however, you are asking yourself probing questions and you really feel peaceful, you may be making a decision based on a truth which you have recognized and, if so, your results will be far better."

As the young man looked back on his life and at his past decisions, he saw dimly that this was true for him. He asked, "How can I learn to make more of my decisions with less effort and anxiety?"

Peter admitted, "I used to be a nervous wreck, like a lot of people in my business, until I learned to develop and trust my own intuition."

"So, how do you do it?" the young man asked.

"I do it first by realizing that my real feelings are 'a personal guide,' a sort of internal mentor, that resides inside of me to show me my own wisdom. I choose to listen to and trust my guiding intuition."

The young man said, "I recall Albert Einstein saying, 'Intuition is the really important thing.'"

"And he was right," Peter said. "Remember, intuition includes not only what you feel about the decision you make, but also what you sense about the way you arrive at your decision."

The young man said, "Lately, I feel anxious because the decision I need to make is complicated."

"Or you believe it is," Peter noted. "You may be using too much ego. A strong ego helps your confidence unless you become egotistical, as though your decision centers solely around you. Even our galaxy is not centered around our earth. And your decision is not usually centered solely around *you.*

"When you become egotistical in a situation, you complicate it. The situation may be complex, of course, but it is only complicated by you."

"What's the difference?" the young man asked.

"*Complex* means there are many parts to the problem," Peter said. "*Complicated* means you cannot distinguish one part from the other.

"If you see a situation as complicated you will remain lost," Peter said. "If you see it as complex and analyze the many parts, you will find several simple, obvious answers. Put them all together and you will have your solution.

"The feeling of fear," Peter continued, "seems complicated until you take it apart. For example, name something you are afraid of."

The young man said, "I'm afraid of flying."

"Take that apart. Are you afraid of flying or are you afraid of crashing?"

He laughed. "I'm afraid of crashing."

"Of course," Peter noted. "All fear is of the future.

"We are not afraid of being *on* a narrow cliff, but of falling *off* the cliff--sometime in the immediate future." Both men smiled.

"When we can honestly see our fear and smile at it we are making progress," Peter said.

He continued, "Reflect on the fearful decisions you have made in your life. Look at those you made based on fear--on insecurity, anxiety, anger, resentment, and worry. All these emotions are the various masks of fear."

While Peter looked out at the view, the young man thought about his own life, and all the decisions he had made based on fear.

Later Peter asked, "What were the results of your fearful decisions?" The young man shook his head, suggesting they had not turned out well.

"You're not alone," Peter said. "For example, do you know anyone who became partners in business dealings or in their personal life who was afraid it would not work out, and who doesn't now regret it?"

"No, I don't," the young man said. "I remember my best friend's marriage. He wasn't sure he loved his girlfriend, but he married her because he was afraid if he didn't, he'd lose her and maybe he'd never find anybody as good again."

"How has it worked out?"

The young man said, "He's divorced."

"I'm very sorry to hear that," Peter said. "Unfortunately, that is the all-too-predictable result of decisions we make based on our fears. We are all afraid, now and then. The secret is not to *act* on fear.

"The good news is we can avoid mistakes if we take the time to ask ourselves, 'What would I do if I were not afraid?' And then *do* whatever that is.

"For example, what do you think would have happened if your friend had not acted on the fear that he would never find anyone else as good to marry?"

The young man said, "He could have broken it off with her and found someone who he felt was more appropriate for him.

"Considering the way the marriage ended," the young man noted, "I'm sure he would have made a better decision if he had acted as though he was not afraid. But he probably didn't take the time to ask himself what he would do if he were not afraid."

"Probably not," Peter agreed.

Then the young man reflected on the decision *he* needed to make and he thought about what he would do if he were not afraid.

He was beginning to make an even better decision.

Then Peter suggested, "Now, think of one of the better decisions you have made in the past."

The young man reviewed his life and grinned as he remembered one of his better decisions.

"Were you afraid then?" Peter asked.

"No, I wasn't afraid."

"Do you see now how your feelings at the time related to the results you got later?" Peter asked.

"I'm beginning to see it," the young man said.

He paused to make a note in his journal:

✓

*My feelings often forecast the consequences.*

✓

"Would you tell me more about intuition?"

Peter answered, "Intuition means being 'in tuition.' *Tuition* comes from the Latin verb *tueri,* meaning 'to watch over.' In medieval times, *tuicion* meant 'protecting.' Today it means teaching."

The young man realized, "Then my intuition protects me by teaching me, based on what has worked for me in the past and what is most likely to work for me now. That makes sense.

"So then, what is my *better* intuition?"

Peter stood up and threw a small stone far out over the gorge. "Do you usually make decisions with your ego or do you get higher guidance?"

The young man smiled and said, "Take a guess." Both men laughed.

Peter said, "There is a better way than relying on ego. When I use this better way, I am not afraid of the world or of myself. I am peaceful. And I make better decisions.

"The concept of 'better intuition' is my own adaptation of The Map," Peter said. "I reserve my better intuition for my most important decisions.

"By 'better intuition,' I mean another kind of intuition--one that gets better results for me. It's what I sense is right for me after I have asked what I call my 'Better Guide' for guidance. It's a source that provides an even greater wisdom for me than my own experience."

The young man asked, "How does someone find this Better Guide?"

"Well, I'll tell you how I find mine, but you may or may not feel it is right for you. You must decide that for yourself.

"If tuition means teaching, intuition is what we have learned *inside* ourselves," Peter said. "Then better intuition is going *beyond* ourselves.

"To do this, I ask for better guidance and then I keep quiet and listen to what comes to me."

The young man realized that many people had been doing this for years through prayer or meditation. Others did it by communing with nature or by simply taking a quiet walk alone.

"*How* you make the decision," Peter said, "certainly influences the decision.

"I ask myself, 'Am I making my decision with fear or enthusiasm?' And I remember that the word *enthusiasm* comes from the Greek *entheos*, which means 'the God within.'"

The young man said, "That reminds me of something I read about fear: 'All fear is simply feeling separated from God.'"

"You are well read," Peter noted. "I have also found that to be true.

"Some people wonder how I stay so calm in the frantic business I'm in," Peter said. "It is because I have learned to use my *intuition* in my everyday decisions and my *better intuition* for my important decisions, especially my personal ones.

"So, what are *you* going to do?" Peter asked. "Are you going to use your intuition and perhaps even your better intuition?

"Don't tell me the answer," Peter suggested. "That's entirely up to you."

Peter added, "Are you familiar with the body's binary code and how it helps you to gain clarity?"

"No, I'm not. How does it work?"

Peter explained, "We think with our minds and feel with our bodies. Our minds can become confused, but our bodies speak to us in a simple binary code: either 'Yes' things feel right to us or 'No' they do not. If you have already used your head by asking yourself the practical question and your answer is still 'Maybe,' then it's time to *feel*, not just think."

Peter said no more. Both men were quiet while the young man reflected on whether or not he really felt good about how he was making his decision.

After a while, the young man thanked Peter and went off to walk along the gorge in silence with his own thoughts. He looked at the huge boulders on the other side and noticed the large magnificent trees lining the far ridge.

Later, after lunch, he and Peter hiked together in mutual silence and respect. They had come to the mountains to enjoy nature and they were absorbing the experience. Late in the afternoon, the young man said, "Peter, I want to thank you very much." Then he went to hike on his own.

Peter waved and called to him in a strong voice, "I wish you well."

Later, when he found himself alone, the young man wrote in his journal:

# My Intuition: A Summary

The more I use my intuition to look at how I feel about <u>how</u> I am making my decision, the more I protect myself from making costly mistakes.

How I feel about how I make a decision often forecasts my results.

I will not make my decision based on fear, as fear has never brought me very good results.

I may make a much better decision when I am guided not by my ego but by my "Better Guide."

Do I feel: Stressed or Peaceful? Clear or Confused? Drained or Energized? Fearful or Enthusiastic? Egotistical or Guided?

What would I decide if I were not afraid?

Does this decision really feel right to me? As right as seeing a favorite color, or meeting a close friend, or taking a peaceful walk?

If it doesn't feel right, it probably isn't, and I need to change my decision. Am I Trusting My Intuition?

I consult my heart by asking myself a private question:

Does My Decision Show I Am Honest with Myself, Trust My Intuition, and Deserve Better?

YES___ OR NO___

√

# My Insight

It was Sunday morning, the last day of The Hike, and the young man had waited until after the sunrise service on the summit to talk with the person he had come to admire most during The Hike.

Nigel "Wings" Macleod was a tall, fit, red-haired Australian who was founder and chairman of a major airline. An approachable man, he still went by his old nickname, Wings. Everyone in the group of hikers gravitated toward him for some reason, and the young man was no exception.

He felt that this man knew what few other people knew, and the young man wanted to learn what he could. When Wings Macleod agreed to talk with him, the young man spoke about what had been bothering him all weekend.

"Sometimes I can sense I am making a poor decision, but I don't seem to care. I just go ahead and make it anyway," the young man admitted.

"Nobody seems to talk about this," he continued. "Am I the only person who does this?"

Wings laughed. "So you want me to talk about what so few people are willing to speak of, do you?"

The young man was taken aback until Wings said, "No worries. I'd be happy to help you discover why you make poor decisions when you know better at the time. But you must be prepared to totally shift gears in your heart to make your own discovery."

The young man said, "I am prepared to do that. I've been asking myself, *'Does My Decision Show I Am Honest with Myself, Trust My Intuition, and Deserve Better?'* What I'm doing has something to do with the last part of this question, doesn't it?"

"It has everything to do with it," Wings said.

"You've told me that you sometimes do things to undermine your own success. That suggests, like most of us, you have to unlearn a belief--that you do not deserve better--that's hidden even from yourself."

"But..." the young man interrupted.

Wings laughed. "I know. You want to interrupt me and tell me that you think you do deserve better. But I am not talking about what you think. I am talking about what you feel--what you really *believe.*

"If you want to discover what you believe, look at what you decide to do--especially what you do often.

"This part about our 'deserving better' is the most difficult for our minds to grasp, but when our hearts feel the truth of it, this insight helps us to soon make better decisions.We just need to look at what we do."

The young man had not expected this. "Can you give me a practical example?" he asked.

"Sure," Wings said. "How often do you make poor decisions because you just don't take the time to get the information you know you need?"

The young man remembered recently doing just that. He grinned and said, "Never. No. Not me!"

Wings laughed. It was good to see that the young man could see his mistakes and laugh at himself.

Wings said, "So you, a bright young lad who knows in his heart that it would be wise to get the information you need, chose not to. Is that correct?"

"Well," he answered, "I wouldn't say 'I chose not to' get the information. I just didn't do it."

Wings asked, "Why would you ever consciously do what you *know* is not in your own best interests?"

The young man did not have a good answer.

"To find your own answer," Wings said, "take a private look at your life. Do you limit your actions to have no more than the success you unknowingly believe you deserve and are comfortable with?

"For example, do you stop at a certain level of success, or happiness, and go no further?

"Do you have a governor in your heart, like the one under the pedal of a rental truck that prevents the driver from going any faster than the maximum speed limit? No matter how hard you press down, on the pedal or on yourself, is the speed of your progress limited by something in the way?"

Wings asked, "Well, what beliefs are you unaware of that get in the way of your actions?

"Would it be all right," he inquired, "if you kept making better decisions, one right after the other? Or would a parade of better decisions take you too far down the road to success or to happiness?

"Even though you probably think it is illogical, could it be that you do not believe you deserve any better? Could your decisions reflect your sabotaging belief, even though you are unaware of it?"

Wings suggested, "Ask yourself, 'Does my decision show me I really believe I deserve better?'"

It was almost too much for the young man to think about. He tried to put it out of his mind.

Both men were quiet.

After a while, the young man asked Wings, "What do you mean by what 'I believe I deserve'?"

Wings said, "Our friend Peter Golden tells me the word *deserve* comes from the Latin word *deservire,* meaning 'to serve zealously.'

"But how many of us serve what is really in our better interests *zealously*? What do *you* really do?

"You may *think* you deserve better, but not *believe* it or act on it. You can resist this truth like one of our great Australian black marlins fighting at the end of a fisherman's line. Most of us fight this idea that we do not *believe* we deserve better.

"But to realize how often it is true, we just need to look at some of our decisions--like your decision not to get the information you knew you needed to get.

"The key to consistently making better decisions," Wings revealed, "is to consciously choose to believe you really deserve better and to act on that belief."

Then Wings rose and said, "You might want to think more about it--or better yet see if you can *feel* the truth of it." Then he went for a walk on his own.

The young man reflected on what he'd heard.

He appreciated being left alone with his thoughts because he knew the question of what he believed he deserved was the most private question of all.

He walked about and pondered, "What do I really believe I deserve?" He was reluctant to see the truth because he didn't always like it. But he continued to look at it. He wondered if he hadn't illogically but unknowingly limited himself and his results.

After a while, he reluctantly pulled out his journal and wrote an important note to reflect upon later:

✓

*We often get the results*
*we unknowingly*
*believe we deserve.*

✓

Later, Wings returned and asked, "Have you been looking at your past decisions--and your beliefs?"

The young man said he had. "I have just begun to appreciate the 'heart' questions you have asked me."

Wings smiled and asked, "When you look at the pattern of your past decisions, what do you notice about what you really believe you deserve?"

To give the young man time to gather his thoughts, Wings said, "Remember, by 'believe' I mean a lot more than what you *think* you deserve.

"Almost everyone consciously thinks they deserve better. But what do you really *believe*?

"Do your actions show you believe you deserve better in every area of your life, both business and personal? If not, why not?" Wings asked.

"Could it be that the world we grow up in encourages us to deny ourselves better? 'Better than what?' people may ask themselves. 'Better than other people?' A caring person would ask, 'Why should I deserve better than others deserve?'

"But that misses the important point," Wings said. "It is not any better than others. It is better than what you are doing to *yourself*. *Everyone* deserves that."

Then Wings was quiet. The young man thought for a moment and then said "I must admit, I guess, sometimes I act as though I don't really believe I deserve any better."

Wings said, "Don't feel badly. I did that too when I was younger. When you were young, did you ever hear this? 'Just *who* ...' he asked, 'do you *think* ...'"

"'You *are*?'" the young man completed.

They both laughed. "I see you've heard that too."

The big Australian asked, "When you were small, how did that make you feel?"

"Small," the young man said with a grin.

"Me too," Wings said. "We can try to laugh it off, but it can stay with us for a long time. That may be why many people seem to hold on to a hidden belief that they deny, even to themselves, that sometimes they really don't deserve any better. Just who do they think they are to deserve better?

"People experience this in various ways. Some do well at work but not at home, or vice versa. As though both successes would be too much. Some carry this hidden belief only at certain times in their lives; others always do because they always deny it."

"Why do we do that?" the young man asked.

"I don't really know," Wings laughed. "All I know is that I keep more on course when I look at what I decide to do and when I ask myself, *'Does My Decision Show I Am Honest with Myself, Trust My Intuition, and Deserve Better?'*

"If my answer is 'No'," Wings noted, "I soon change my decision and then I change my behavior.

"I have built a successful airline with the help of other people," Wings said, "by encouraging all of us in our organization to act on our own belief that we each deserve better."

The young man realized that Wings focused not just on changing what he believed, but on what he *did*. And he helped others to do the same.

Then the young man privately asked himself, "What do I believe, and what do I do?"

The young man asked himself, "Before I make a decision, do I usually ask myself valuable questions? Do I focus on the real need instead of what I want? Do I get the needed information and inform myself of my options? Do I think my decision through to better results?

"Or do I not really believe that I deserve better and therefore sabotage myself by not telling myself the truth? Or by not trusting my own intuition? Or by believing I do not have the ability to do better, or enough education, or the right social connections?"

Wings spoke quietly to the young man, who had been deep in his thoughts. "We never let ourselves have any more than we really believe we deserve."

Then Wings asked, "Are you driving with your brakes on?" The young man looked up.

"What do you mean?"

"I mean, are you slowing yourself down by believing you deserve to merely survive rather than prosper?"

Wings said, "Don't tell me. Tell yourself."

Again, the young man's mind wanted to avoid the conversation--to escape the discomfort he felt.

Then he began to wonder, "What *do* I really believe?"

After he thought about it, the young man said, "May I ask you something?"

The Australian laughed. "Why stop now?"

The young man had to laugh. Then he asked, "What can I do if I realize I do not really believe I deserve better?" the young man asked.

"That's a great question," Wings said.

"Ask yourself, 'If I believed I deserved better results, what would I do?'

"You do not need to wait until you really believe it in your heart. You just need to *do* now whatever you would do if you did believe you deserved better.

"When your actions are better, things get better.

"Remember, decisions are only effective when you act on them," Wings said. "And when you act on them *in time.*

"For example, you might ask yourself, 'Do I believe in my decision enough to act on it, *soon*?'"

Just then, the other hikers came over to talk. Wings, the young man, and the others spent another hour sitting on the summit, looking out at the spectacular view, thinking, talking, and enjoying one another's company. They were all enjoying The Hike.

When things quieted down, the young man thanked Wings and quietly slipped away to make some important notes.

Before he went looking for the guide, with whom he wanted to make the descent, he wrote in his journal. He wanted to remember these insights into his beliefs about his personal worth, and how they unknowingly affected his decisions.

## My Insight: A Summary

My decisions are affected by my beliefs, especially about what I really believe I deserve.

To discover what I really believe, I look closely at what I most often <u>do</u>.

I may <u>think</u> I deserve better, but my actions show me that sometimes I do not really <u>believe</u> I do.

The key to my consistently making better decisions is to choose to believe I deserve better & then to act on that belief.

Have I looked closely enough at my past decisions & actions to discover what I <u>really</u> believe I deserve? Do I see how my decisions reveal my beliefs? Do I believe enough in my decision to act on it soon? What would I decide to do now if I really believed I deserved better?

I consult my heart by asking myself a private question:

*Does My Decision Show I Am Honest with Myself, Trust My Intuition, and Deserve Better?*

YES___ OR NO___

## A Review

As the hikers descended the mountain, the young man hiked down with the guide. They reviewed what he had learned the last few days.

The guide asked, "When you look back at where you began this journey on Friday, what do you see?"

The young man said, "I see that the way I arrived at The Hike on Friday was not unlike the way I was making many of my decisions. I didn't realize that I was headed in the wrong direction. I didn't have the needed information--the directions showing me how to get here. I didn't inform myself of my options. And when I decided to leave home without the directions, I didn't think my decision through.

"I was just fooling myself. I felt I should go back and get the directions, but I ignored my feelings--my intuition. Maybe, at some level, I didn't feel I deserved to get any better results, because I've made the same kind of mistakes before, but I hadn't learned from them."

The guide said, "How do you feel now?"

"I feel more awake," the young man smiled.

"I made my own version of The Map with the thoughts and questions. Now I carry it in my wallet."

The guide smiled and said, "Of course, you know the key will be to do more than carry The Map with you. You will need to take it out and *use* it often.

"When you do, you will make better decisions."

"That's what happened to me this weekend."

"What happened?" the guide asked.

"Well, I did what you suggested. First, I took a personal inventory and wrote down my initial decision. Then I asked myself the two questions.

"First I asked, *'Am I Meeting the Real Need, Informing Myself of Options, and Thinking It Through?'* Initially I answered a quick 'Yes' to this question, because I thought it was my true answer.

"Then I asked, *'Does My Decision Show I Am Honest with Myself, Trust My Intuition, and Deserve Better?'* and I discovered I was just fooling myself.

"I'm glad you encouraged me to be patient, because after I asked myself the private question, I saw that when I went back and asked myself the practical question again, I made a far better decision.

"I saw things differently--more clearly."

"What did you see?" the guide asked.

"First, I saw I was pursuing what I wanted, not what was really needed. Second, I really hadn't gathered the needed information. And third, I certainly hadn't thought my decision all the way through to the results I needed.

"As I said, after asking the *private* 'heart' question, it helped me to go back and honestly use my head and my heart to make a far better decision.

"I just wrote down my better decision a few minutes ago on the inventory sheet and compared it with the initial decision I was probably going to make before I came on The Hike. It's *better!*

"I've definitely made a much better decision.

"And I am going to ask myself the two questions again and see if I can make an even better decision over the next few days.

"Although, as you say, it may already be good enough to have simply made a better decision."

The guide smiled. "You have taught yourself a great deal. You should feel good about yourself."

"Yes, I do. I'm also glad you encouraged me to talk with the other hikers and to listen to them and to myself. And as I wrote out my own Map, it helped me to discover for myself what I needed to learn."

The guide asked, "When you are on your own, will you remember to ask yourself the questions and use your head and heart to make your decision?"

The young man said, "Hopefully, I will remember to ask myself the questions as often as I need to."

Then he thanked the guide profusely, and went to thank the others. He waited, however, as he found them making the descent in a reflective mood. He realized they, too, were reviewing their decisions.

When each hiker had reached the lower level at his or her own pace, the group met to say their good-byes. Then he thanked each of them. Some shook hands, others hugged. They all felt a kinship.

He asked, "How can I thank you all?"

Ingrid said, "That's easy. Use it. And help *others* use it as well." He smiled and promised he would.

Later, they parted friends.

As he hiked alone along the trail at the base of the mountain heading for his car, the young man looked back on what he had learned and he looked ahead to how he would use it every day.

He would take the time to ask himself the two questions before he made any substantial decision.

Later, when he returned to his office, he simplified his handwritten Map, had it typed up, and then reduced it to the size of a credit card, so he could carry The Map in his wallet and *use* it regularly.

# The Map

*To a Better Decision*

---

### "YES" or "NO"
#### THE MAP TO A BETTER DECISION

*I avoid indecision & half-decisions based on half-truths.*

*I use **both** halves of a reliable system to consistently make better decisions: a cool head and a warm heart.*

### I USE MY HEAD
*by asking myself a practical question.*

### <u>AND</u>

### I CONSULT MY HEART
*by asking myself a private question.*

*Then, after I listen to myself and others, I make a better decision and act on it.*

---

TO USE MY HEAD, I ASK A PRACTICAL QUESTION:

### AM I MEETING THE REAL NEED, INFORMING MYSELF OF OPTIONS, AND THINKING IT THROUGH?

#### "YES"__ OR "NO"__

Is it a mere want or a real need? What information do I need? Have I created options? If I did "x," then what would happen? Then what?

TO CONSULT MY HEART, I ASK A PRIVATE QUESTION:

### DOES MY DECISION SHOW I AM HONEST WITH MYSELF, TRUST MY INTUITION, AND DESERVE BETTER?

#### "YES"__ OR "NO"__

Am I telling myself the truth? Does this feel right? What would I decide if I wasn't afraid? What would I do if I deserved better?

IF "YES" I PROCEED    IF "NO" I RETHINK

#### WHAT IS MY BETTER DECISION?

✓

## *In Use*

Several months later, the young man knew he was no longer just a young man, but had matured into a man. As he sat in his office, the man realized he had assumed the responsibility of making far better decisions at work and in his personal life.

He had carried The Map in his wallet and used it whenever he needed to reach a better decision.

It wasn't long before people noticed the change. He was more confident and decisive. He calmly asked more questions and he listened more.

Several people asked him what had happened. When they heard about the simple "Yes" or "No" System he was using, they asked to know more.

He shared his notes from The Hike with those who were really interested, and he encouraged them to make their own Map. They, in turn, used the System and showed others how to use it.

Now, the man was waiting for some of the people he worked with to soon join him in his office.

When the meeting began, he asked, "Would it be useful for us to meet for one hour once a week and look, as a team, at how we can make better decisions? It would all be on a voluntary basis.

"Each of us could use the two questions during the week for our own decisions. Then we might review our departmental decisions, as a group, at ten o'clock every Thursday morning. We might discover where we can, together, make even better decisions.

"Is this something you would find valuable?"

One of his colleagues exclaimed, "Yes!"

She laughed and added, "I'm in favor of it because I forget to use the questions, even though I know they work." Others nodded in agreement.

"But if I knew we were going to be meeting, it would motivate me to ask myself the questions, and I think I would make better decisions."

They all agreed, and later they held their first weekly decision meeting. The meeting, like the others that followed, began with them asking, *"Are We Meeting the Real Need, Informing Ourselves of Options, and Thinking It Through?"*

After a few meetings, practically everyone arrived better prepared, as they knew they would be discussing what they had wanted to do and how they had since discovered what the real need was.

They asked each other to describe the needed results so clearly that they could all see the better results as though they were already happening.

They explained to each other the pros and cons of at least three options, and why they chose one as more likely to help them meet the real need.

They asked themselves, "Then what would happen?" and they outlined what they expected to happen, step-by-step, until they reached the needed results, with a specified timetable for each phase.

At first, some people felt uneasy asking the private question aloud. So they asked it only of themselves.

Eventually, more people took a lighthearted approach, smiled, and asked, "Ah ha, but are we telling ourselves *the truth*?" or "But does this really *feel right* in our hearts?" or "But what would we decide if we really believed we *deserved* better?"

They enjoyed themselves more as they laughed together, but as each person privately examined his or her thoughts and feelings, the group's decisions improved. They made better decisions working together than any one of them would have made on their own.

They had avoided the mediocrity of weak compromise, so common in groups, by working as clear, cooperative individuals.

They soon realized the group was making its own decisions and that the man was only guiding them.

As the news spread of the weekly "Yes" or "No" meetings, people noticed that those who attended were given more freedom to make decisions. They got better results and would get promotions. Before long, some of the skeptical people who had not chosen to attend the meetings asked to join in.

Soon, several departments were having their own "Yes" or "No" sessions each week.

People often wanted to meet for longer than an hour, but they soon learned they had to come well prepared with their answers because, for efficiency, the meetings were never extended beyond an hour.

Just knowing that they would be discussing their decisions, and the way they were making their decisions, prompted many people to ask themselves the two questions regularly throughout the week.

Over the years, the organization and the people prospered. The man realized that his business teams were now made up of more decisive people. And the man remembered how it all came about.

# The Personal Guide

*Two Years Later*

$A$s he sat in his new corner office two years later, the man realized how far he had come. He was now less naive and more aware of what was going on around him and within him.

The guide and other hikers had said, "In each of us resides 'a guide' who is an internal mentor that each of us is given to show us our own wisdom.

"Our guide is ourself."

The man smiled. He saw that his challenge was to say "Yes" to reality and "No" to illusions.

He would continue to use his head to ask probing questions and his heart to find better answers.

He would stay focused on the real need, personally gather or verify needed information, and become more aware of his options. He would think each of his options through and gain better results.

He realized he could more easily distinguish reality from illusion when he told himself the truth, trusted his better intuition, and acted on the belief that he deserved better.

What had seemed complicated to him remained complex, but it was now clear that, when he used a better system, he made better decisions. He was glad he had done more than just learn the questions; he had learned to *use* them regularly.

He now felt personally renewed and enjoyed a prosperity and peacefulness he had not known in his earlier years.

The man got up and began to pace about his office. He was looking forward to a special meeting with the guide, whom he had not seen since The Hike.

It had been a good journey two years ago, for along the way he had met a better part of himself.

He felt better than ever about his future. Since he had introduced the "Yes" or "No" System, he had seen improvement in organizational morale and profits. And he was prospering himself.

The guide said as he entered the office, "I have been hearing great things about you and your company."

The man smiled. "Thank you. Remember what you told me? 'The System works best when you *use* it.' Well, we really *use* it here." They both laughed.

The man added, "The people here who get in the habit of using their heads and their hearts to discover better answers *do* get better results. The more they use The System, the better they do, and so does our organization. So much for my little speech."

The guide laughed. "How would you feel about you and I sharing this with other organizations?"

The man said, "I would be happy to help."

Then they agreed to work together to develop better ways to apply the System and to get the information to more people. They discussed several ideas, including distributing information about the "Yes" or "No" System to the company's customers and potential customers to help them make their own better decisions, hopefully in the company's favor.

Eventually, after planning to meet again soon, they shook hands and the guide left.

The man was now alone with his thoughts.

He wished he had learned to make better decisions even earlier in his life, as it would have made quite a difference. He was glad he had started to work with others to get this information to youngsters in the neighborhood schools, so they could use it sooner in life. He thought, "The sooner we learn to make better decisions, the sooner we get better results.

"If we all made better decisions at work and at home, everyone in our families, our organizations, and our communities could all benefit."

Then he realized that, as useful as he was to his company and to his community, he was even more pleased with what had happened at home.

He and members of his family had learned to ask themselves the practical "head" question and the private "heart" question, and to listen to the better part of themselves before they made their decisions.

And they were all now a lot happier.

The more he thought about it, the more he saw how valuable it was for people to make better decisions in their personal lives, and to help those they cared about to see how they could do the same.

The man looked at the special paperweight on his desk which displayed the two questions that reminded him to use a cool head and a warm heart when he made his decisions.

He smiled, again recalling what the guide had said: "The System works best when you *use* it."

He noticed that because he was *using* a reliable system, he could more quickly and easily say "Yes" to what worked well and "No" to what did not. And he knew that by consistently making better decisions he had earned a better life. Then he grinned.

He realized:

✓

We are each our own guide
to better decisions.

And we can help others
discover this as well.

✓

the end

✓